# Kara Walker: White Shadows in Blackface

Robert Hobbs

Karma

# Table of Contents

# Introduction

Among the most celebrated artists of the past three decades, Kara Walker (b. 1969) is known for her tough, critical, provocative, and highly imaginative representations of African Americans and whites reaching back to antebellum times. In 1994, the same year the Rhode Island School of Design awarded her an MFA, her fifty-foot installation of black cut-paper silhouettes was shown at the Drawing Center in New York. Entitled *Gone: An Historical Romance of a Civil War as It Occurred b'tween the Dusky Thighs of One Young Negress and Her Heart*, this mural was a huge critical success, and it inaugurated a stellar career presently totaling ninety-three one-person exhibitions, including a major survey organized in 2007 by the Walker Art Center, Minneapolis, which subsequently traveled to ARC/Musée d'art moderne de la ville de Paris and the Whitney Museum of American Art, New York. In 1997, Walker was awarded the John D. and Catherine T. MacArthur Foundation Achievement Award, and in 2021, she became a member of the American Academy of Arts and Letters.

I was first introduced to Walker's work in 1995 by the prescient collector and art advisor Suzanne Feldman, who had acquired several of the artist's early works, including pieces from her MFA exhibition. Soon thereafter, I had the opportunity to view Walker's second Wooster Gardens show and to meet Brent Sikkema, the gallery's founder, and its director, Michael Jenkins (later a partner of Sikkema Jenkins & Co.). Jenkins had studied art with Kara's father, Larry Walker, at the Atlanta College of Art, and both he and the gallery have consequently enjoyed a special relationship with her. After seeing several shows of Walker's work and attending her insightful lecture at Virginia Commonwealth University, in which she emphasized the insanity of the stereotypical figures appearing in her work, I proposed showing her work at the São Paulo Bienal. Wishing to respect the many challenges Walker's art presents, my proposal included the 1997 mural of black cut-paper silhouettes entitled *Slavery! Slavery! Presenting a GRAND and LIFELIKE Panoramic Journey into Picturesque Southern Slavery or "Life at 'Ol' Virginny's Hole' (sketches from Plantation Life)"* as well as her 1998 works *Cut* and *Letter from a Black Girl*. Because these are demanding pieces, requiring viewers to become aware of the almost insurmountable problems that can ensue when African Americans internalize white racists' stereotypical views of Blacks, the selection committee decided this exhibition would provide an accurate picture of this artist's work and chose it to represent the United States at the 2002 São Paulo Bienal.

Over the years, there have been a great many critical reviews as well as a number of monographs on Walker's work, but the highly provocative nature of her art has tended to take precedence over contextual and historical analyses. Thus, my early investigation of Walker's work for the Bienal catalogue and my essay for the subsequent catalogue (also published in 2002) for her show at Kunstverein Hannover continue to be among the more in-depth investigations of her challenging and stirring art. Specifically, these extended essays consider its five main sources: blackface Americana, Harlequin Romance novels, Julia Kristeva's theory of abjection, Stone Mountain's racist tourist attraction, and the minstrel tradition. I fortunately recognized almost immediately that art as confrontational and mature as Walker's could not have been created in a vacuum; instead, it had to be predicated on a number of fully developed traditions. The main questions were: Which traditions prepared Walker for her radical work? And how can they be understood as informing the direction her art has taken? My intention was to place Walker's contributions within the historical perspectives that enable us to better understand it; thus, I strove to underscore not only her art's historical relevancy but also its enduring cogency, since it transposed into fine art a range of highly political, low-brow literary, demandingly theoretical, and particularly racist sources.

Because the State Department does not permit distribution in the United States of catalogues it finances for international venues, and because Kunstverein Hannover has not focused on marketing its Kara Walker catalogue, making it difficult even for me to obtain copies, my two extended essays on Walker—the focus of this Karma publication—will for the first time be receiving widespread distribution in the United States and abroad.

Any art historical undertaking willingly incurs debts to members of the art world, including gallerists, museum professionals, and fellow scholars, and I am delighted to acknowledge the wonderful help I have received from a number of individuals. At Sikkema Jenkins & Co., it has been a great pleasure over the years to know and rely on the advice of Brent Sikkema and Michael Jenkins, who each have a profound appreciation and understanding of art. More recently, I have been pleased to work with two of the gallery's experts, Meg Malloy and Monica Truong, who have been most helpful in providing images of Walker's work. My essays have benefited from the perceptive reading provided by distinguished African and African American scholar Dr. Babatunde Lawal and from conversations with the extraordinary critic, curator, and scholar of contemporary and African American art Dr. Lowery Stokes Sims, who has been a great friend. Dr. Vittorio Colaizzi, who was then the Thalhimer Graduate Assistant at Virginia Commonwealth University, was indefatigable in following up the many leads and questions I posed in the course of researching Walker's art. He also served as a respected sounding board for the ideas I developed, as did Jean Crutchfield, a keen critic. I am particularly pleased that Walker read both essays and found them germane.

She also provided several additional pieces of information that have helped to round out this study.

My sincere thanks go to Brendan Dugan, founder of Karma Books, who has recognized the continued relevancy of the texts now composing *Kara Walker: White Shadows in Blackface*, as well as David Schoerner, publications director, who has thoughtfully and conscientiously overseen the production of this book. Designer Paige Hanserd has created a most sympathetic design; copy editor Miles Champion and Amelia Farley have served as assiduous editors. Together, these individuals have formed a most congenial team in making this book a reality.

I have had the great fortune to work with Alison Hagge on a number of books. As in the past, she has been unfailingly excellent in her editorial suggestions and in her overall commitment to excellence.

Finally, I wish to express my deep appreciation to two discerning collectors, Lewis Manilow and Peter Norton, who have believed in this project from the beginning, and to Sharon Helgason Gallagher, president and publisher of Artbook/D.A.P., for her long-term interest in both Walker's art and my research on this artist.

—Robert Hobbs

# Kara Walker's
# *Slavery! Slavery!*

*This 2002 essay was published for the exhibition of the same name, which was the official US representative at the twenty-fifth São Paulo Bienal. Because the State Department's official policy is not to permit the catalogues it publishes to be distributed in the United States, this piece is little known outside of Brazil.*

—R.H.

*Race, as a meaningful criterion within the biological sciences, has long been recognized to be a fiction. When we speak of "the white" or "the black race," "the Jewish race" or "the Aryan race," we speak in biological misnomers and more generally, in metaphors. . . . Race, in these usages, pretends to be an objective term of classification, when in fact it is a dangerous trope. . . . Race is the ultimate trope of difference because it is so very arbitrary in its application.*

Henry Louis Gates Jr., *"Race," Writing, and Difference*, 1986

"Contemptible collectibles," "blackface Americana," "Black memorabilia," and "anti-Black artifacts" are the terms most often used for the antiques and recently produced objects that are known by these different categories, depending on one's reaction to them. Sometimes the word *racist* is added to reinforce their original demeaning intent, but increasingly these articles that continue to stereotype African Americans in terms of exaggerated features and controversial activities are becoming known under the simple, straightforward rubric "Black collectibles." The noncommittal stance indicated by this term is appropriate since these tchotchkes, which range from late nineteenth-century pieces to recently manufactured ones, from trading cards to cookie jars, mechanical banks, and cast-iron groom hitching posts (to name only a few of a much larger group of object types), have elicited a number of heated responses after becoming eagerly sought-after items in the past two decades by such notables as Julian Bond, Bill Cosby, Whoopi Goldberg, Bobby Short, and Mike Tyson.

In *Images in Black: 150 Years of Black Collectibles*, market specialist Douglas Congdon-Martin estimates that 70 percent of this material is regularly purchased by African Americans, who acquire Black memorabilia because of a desire to understand their history, even to the extent of wishing to comprehend how these racist stereotypes have contributed to it. He goes on to say that some Blacks and whites buy these objectionable pieces with the express purpose of removing them from view. Some whites find them strangely nostalgic and even comforting, evidently assuming, with an alarming naivete and a specious form of reasoning, that the sins of the past are permissible if they have contributed to our present state of affairs. Given this range of attitudes, it is not surprising that still others collect examples of these long-invoked stereotypes because they are seeking confirmation of their racist views.[1]

A brief history of the acquisition and display of Black collectibles is crucial to an understanding of the art of African American artist Kara Walker since it enables us to appreciate conflicted attitudes developing in the wake of both civil rights legislation and political correctness policies that provide a basis for her work. Only months after receiving an MFA from the Rhode Island School of Design, Walker impressed members of the New York art world with an imposing fifty-foot mural at the Drawing Center that she titled, as a send-up of Margaret Mitchell's famous novel, *Gone: An Historical Romance of a Civil War as It Occurred b'tween the Dusky Thighs of One Young Negress and Her Heart*. Apropos this exhibition, *New York Times* art critic Holland Cotter commented:

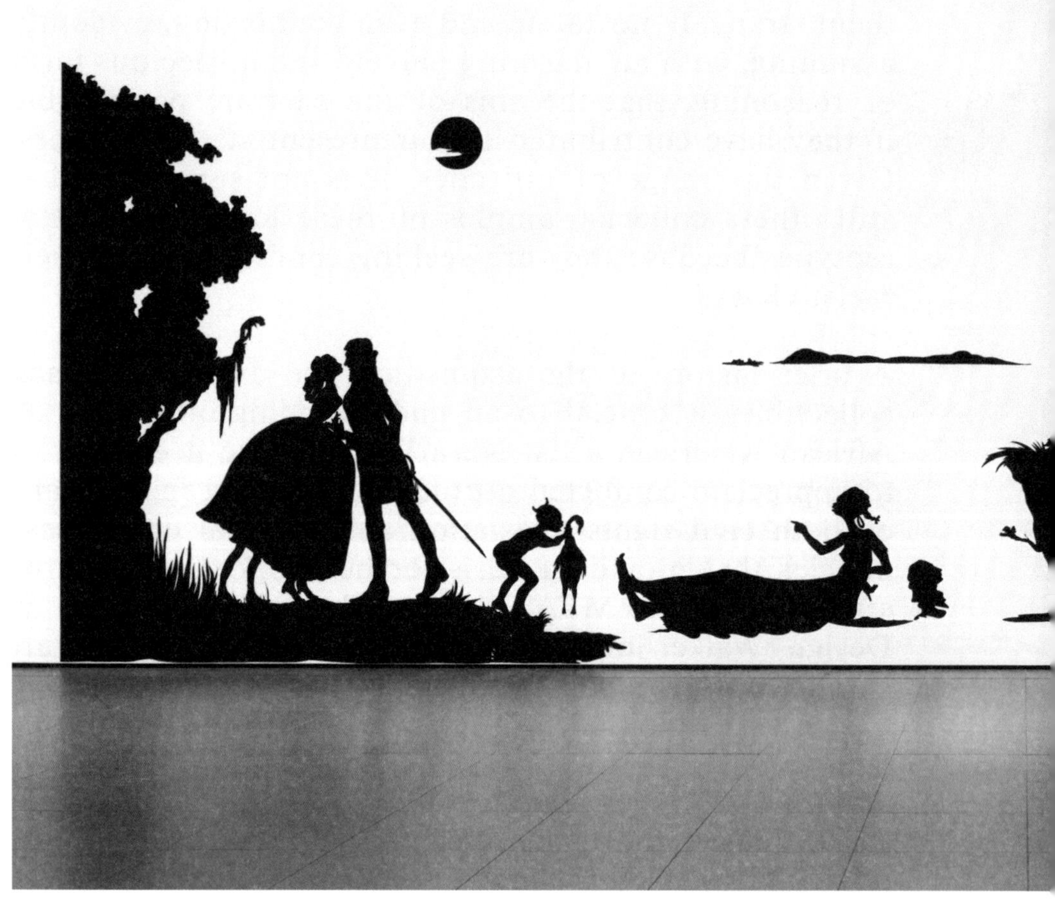

Kara Walker, *Gone: An Historical Romance of a Civil War as It Occurred b'tween the Dusky Thighs of One Young Negress and Her Heart*, 1994, cut paper and adhesive on wall, 156 × 600 inches (396.2 × 1,524 cm) overall

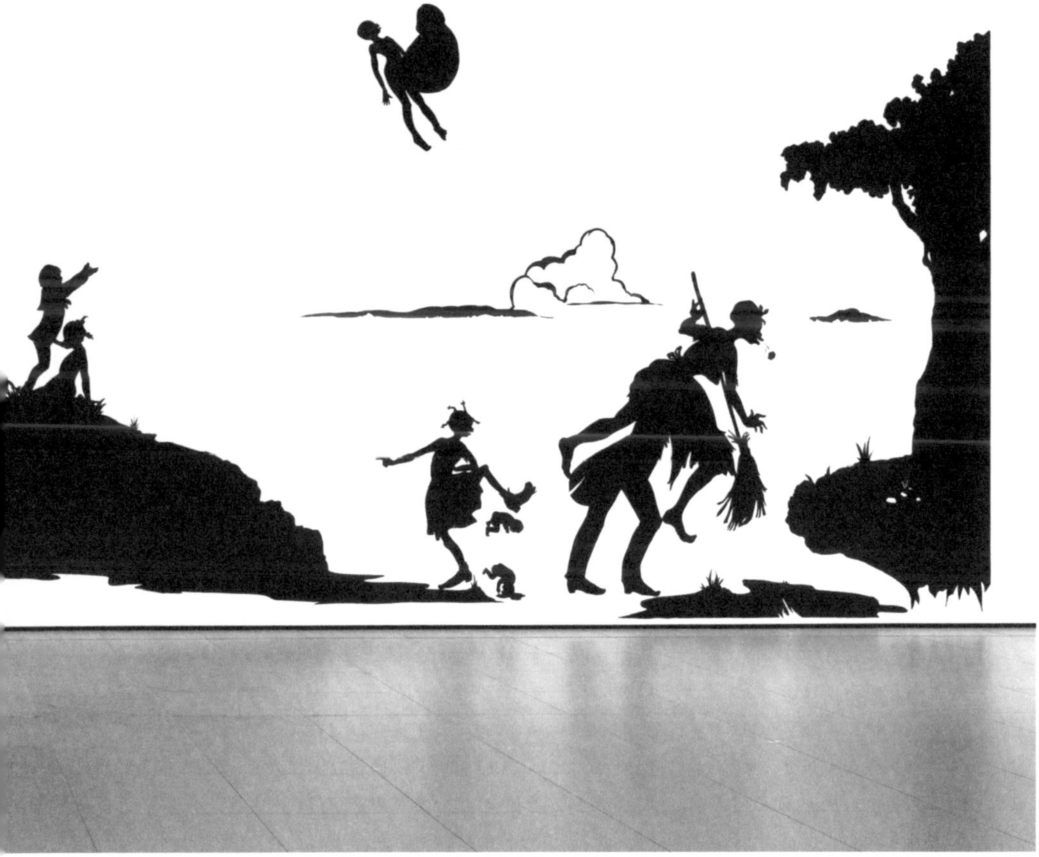

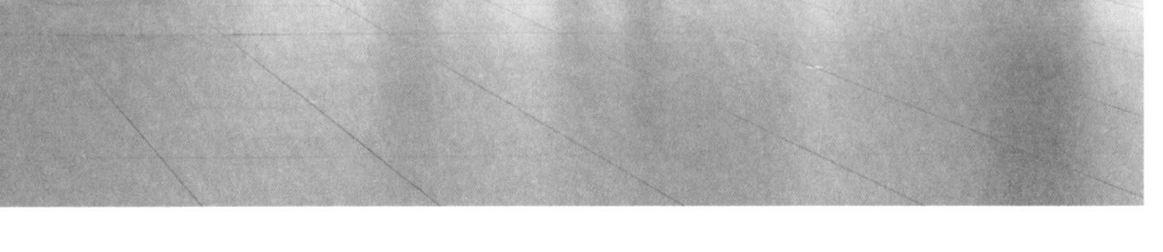

Collection of the Museum of Modern Art, New York. Gift of The Speyer Family Foundation in honor of Marie-Josée Kravis. Digital Image © The Museum of Modern Art/Licensed by SCALA / Art Resource, NY

> Kara Walker explores drawing's narrative potential in a large figurative tableau that looks as if it were drawn in ink but is actually made of silhouettes cut from black paper. This technique, popular for making quick, inexpensive portraits in the last century, is decisively updated in Ms. Walker's hands as she fashions a surreal, raunchy, angry fantasia on the world of antebellum slavery. Looking like a cross between a children's book and a sexually explicit cartoon, this is skillful, imaginative work and will doubtless be showing up elsewhere soon.[2]

Although Walker's work immediately attracted a wide following, critics have regularly noted that neither the whites nor the Blacks represented in it are characterized as winners. In the eight years since its New York debut, Walker's art, however, has proven particularly offensive to civil rights–era Blacks who have availed themselves of the modern propensity to essentialize and reify identity in their ongoing battle against racist images by creating paragons of African American morality in their art. Viewing the world in terms of a blurring of binary oppositions, Walker's new hybrid and even incestuous couplings of both Black and white stereotypes have made some members of this generation uneasy. Although her art has not been viewed in terms of the relatively recent post–civil rights fascination with Black collectibles by upscale African Americans, it is in part predicated on the reevaluation of this material.

The first acknowledged gallery exhibition of Black memorabilia was the 1982 show *Ethnic Notions* at the Berkeley Art Center, Berkeley University, which featured the collection of Janette Faulkner, an African American social worker who began acquiring blackface objects in the early 1960s.[3] In her statement regarding reasons for building such

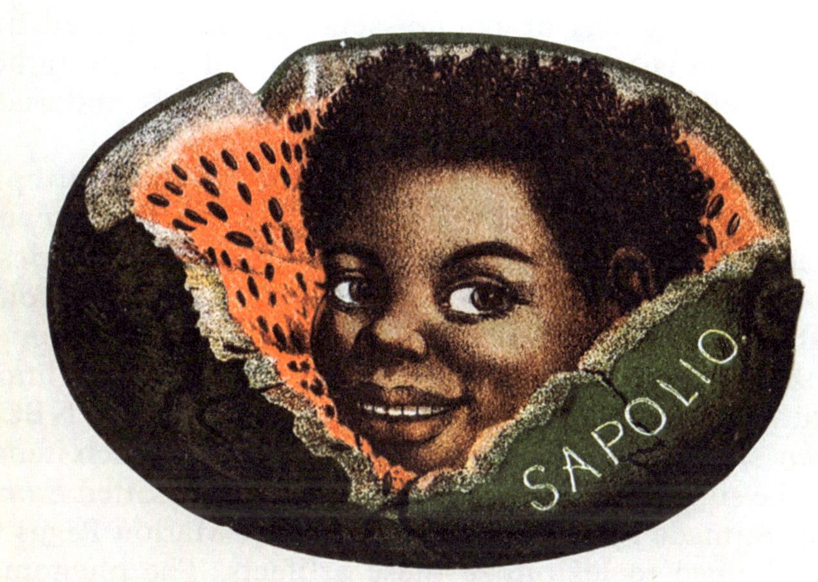


*Ethnic Notions: Black Images in the White Mind*, 1982. This catalogue corresponded with an exhibition at the Berkeley Art Center, Berkeley University

a collection, Faulkner described her initial shock at finding in an antique shop a postcard picturing a stereotypical view of a man with missing teeth that bore the caption, "dares mo laak dis back home."[4] Faulkner explained that collecting and living with such objects over the years strengthened her ability to cope with racial prejudice by providing her with a historical perspective. Moreover, studying large quantities of this material enabled her to gain a needed aesthetic distance from it, since she acquired over time the tempering lens of connoisseurship that enabled her to focus on issues of style, technique, and quality rather than dwell only on the subject matter of this material.[5]

Although Faulkner deserves high marks for her intrepid collecting tastes and for challenging herself to live with objects whose original intent was to poke fun at African Americans by demeaning them, such exemplary stoutheartedness only partially explains how the acquisition of these objects soon became fashionable among Black luminaries and professionals. Faulkner's appearance on NBC's *Today* show quickly spread the idea of owning such items, and the sixty-minute documentary film, also entitled *Ethnic Notions*, made by independent filmmaker Marlon Riggs in 1987 helped to legitimize these artifacts. The phenomenon became so widespread in the 1980s that it generated a quarterly magazine called *Black Ethnic Collectibles* and a national group named the Black Memorabilia Collectors Association (BMCA), which, in 1990 boasted thirteen local chapters in metropolitan areas throughout the United States, a membership of more than 700 people, and even an active youth component that served college, secondary, and elementary students.

But collecting Black memorabilia became much more than rigorous acts of valor that intimately acquainted collectors with objects able to steel them for adversity by reminding them that blatantly open acts of prejudice have been permitted, and even encouraged, in the past. Even though collectors of Black memorabilia have regularly taken refuge in the rationale that they are buying history, a keen and assiduous appreciation for past reality, extending even to its darker aspects, is in retrospect not the main reason for pursuing this material. In *Ethnic Notions*, Robbin Henderson, director of the Berkeley Art Center, provides an answer by pointing out unequivocally, "This is not a collection of artifacts about black history. Most of this material was created by white people. It is the consciousness of the dominant class which we see in this collection."[6] The practice of collecting blackface memorabilia has thus become enormously empowering to Blacks since these artifacts are now being seen as an ongoing indictment of racist white attitudes that have materialized as racist Americana. As Erskine Peters, then an assistant professor of Afro-American Studies at Berkeley, opines:

> Perhaps the [white] artificers of these images never really considered that they were preserving and projecting what was actually a gulf within themselves more than outside of themselves. Perhaps, too, most of these artificers never considered that the figures should have been cast in white instead of blackface.[7]

Peters concludes that blackface memorabilia is far more incriminating of whites, who created and originally purchased these images, than of Blacks, who were in turn subjected to the racist attitudes giving rise to these objects. While the Emancipation Proclamation was enacted as law by Abraham Lincoln at the end of the Civil War and full passage of civil rights legislation became a reality a century later, the equally difficult work of disinterring and critiquing the ideological morass attending slavery and segregation has only begun to be undertaken by African Americans on a broad basis in the past few decades. Janette Faulkner may well be the Rosa Parks of the current war on racist ideology, but the battle against its long-term effects is just beginning.

In a 1981 letter, written no doubt to the National Endowment for the Humanities, which helped support this exhibition, poet and novelist Alice Walker articulated the terms of this ideological battle that has not only pitted Blacks against whites but also created dissension among Blacks. In her letter, Alice Walker establishes the parameters of this war on ideology. Even though her thoughts were unknown to Kara Walker when she was maturing as an artist, this same rationale has become crucially important to her work. Alice Walker writes:

> These caricatures and stereotypes were really intended as prisons. Prisons without the traditional bars, but prisons of image. Inside each desperately grinning "sambo" and each placid 300-pound "mammy" lamp there is imprisoned a real person, someone we know. If you look hard at the collection and don't panic . . . you will begin to really see, the eyes and then the hearts of these despised relatives of ours, who have been forced to lock their true spirits away from themselves and away from us. . . .
>
> This is the way I now see Jan Faulkner's collection. I see our brothers and sisters, mothers and fathers, captured and forced into images they did not devise, doing hard time for all of us.
>
> We can liberate them by understanding this. And free ourselves.[8]

Being "captured and forced into images they did not devise" is, according to Alice Walker, being forced into a stereotypical role, a particularly insidious and long-lasting form of slavery —a doubling of slavery akin to the title of Kara Walker's panorama, as we will see—that continues to the present.

Our familiarity with stereotypes does not equip us to understand the dynamics of how they entrap their subjects. Because of ideology's chameleonlike ability to assume the look of reality, its capacity for subsuming stereotypes under the guise of "the natural" has proven more insidious than one might expect. Alice Walker's reference to the word *capture* in her letter suggests an important clue for unraveling the workings of stereotypical images. Firmly established in the annals of Black cultural studies, the received wisdom regarding these images is in part derived from the prescient thought of the expatriate Martiniquais psychiatrist, theorist, and revolutionary Frantz Fanon. In his widely read *Black Skin, White Masks*, Fanon employs Jacques Lacan's well-known 1938 recasting of Sigmund Freud's theory of identity formation in terms of ongoing paranoia as a basis for his own discussion of the type of problems that result from perpetuating racial stereotypes. Fanon substantially rethinks Lacan's imaginary realm by bumping it up to a level that focuses on the way entire social groups, consisting of individuals, each undergoing a similar process, can be held hostage by an image. In the process, Fanon apparently conflated aspects of Lacan's symbolic order, designating the world into which one is born with his imaginary order since they are viewed dynamically as desired or (perhaps, more realistically) necessary images in the structuring of an ego consistent with the dominant social order. Known as the mirror stage, Lacan's theory focuses on the alienation of self that comes from a child basing his or her identity on an external mirror image or another person. Even though the

Pages 25–27: Kara Walker, *Slavery! Slavery!* (details)

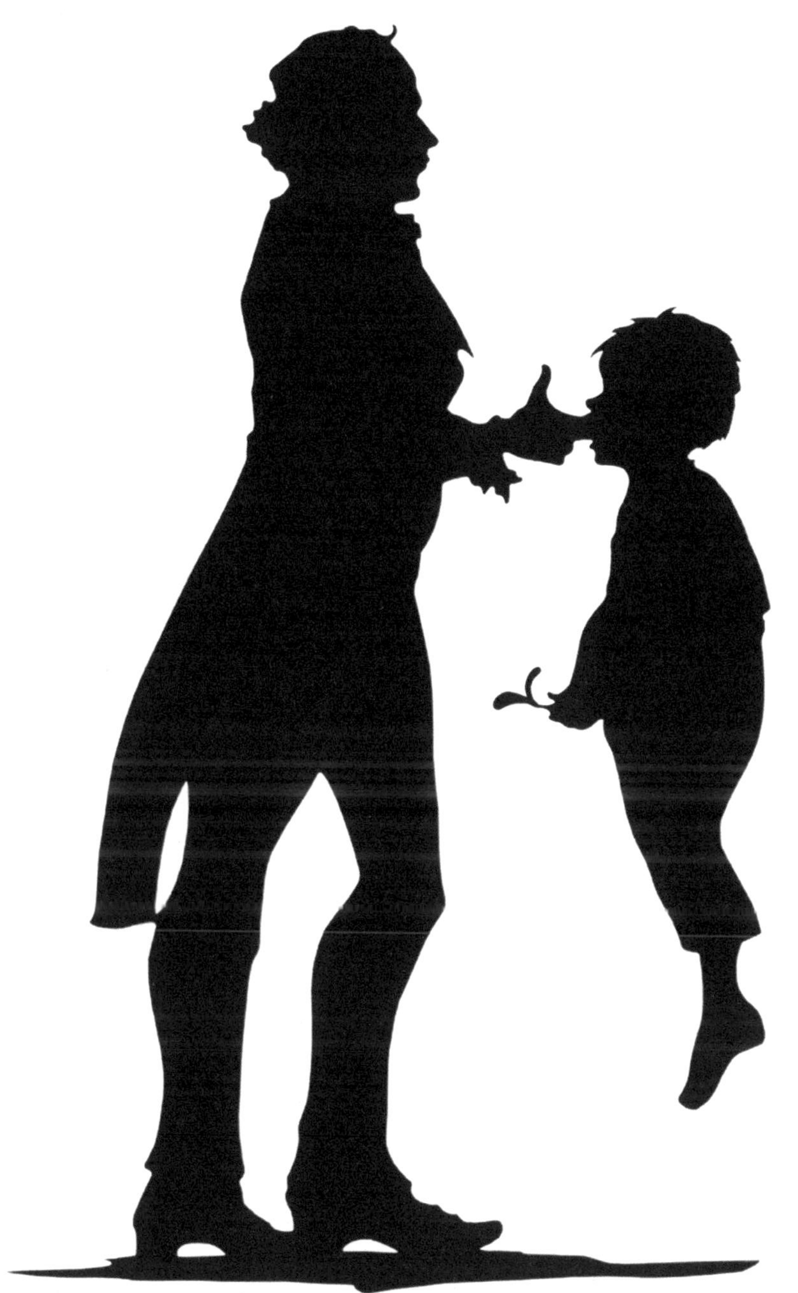

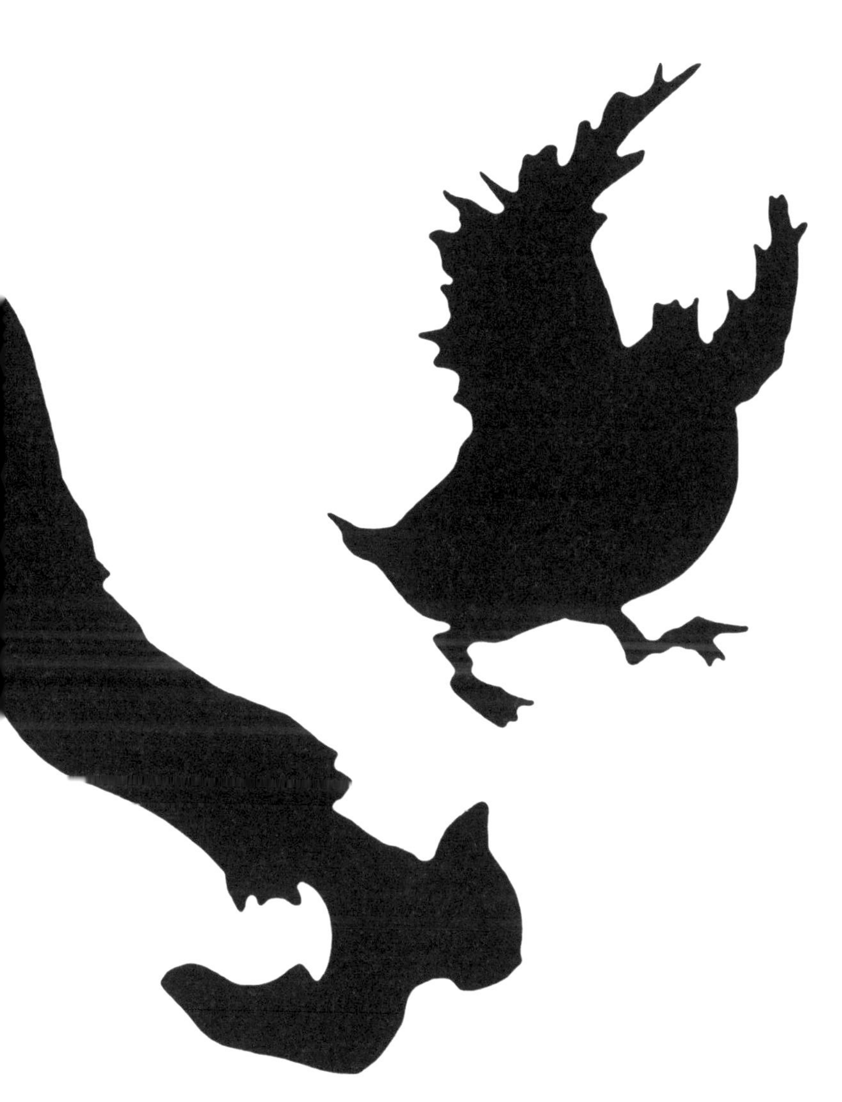

mirror stage references the first occurrence of this process of ego formation through disjunction, the process can be reformulated in terms of an entire social group, as Alice Walker's reference to the fact that, in the past, racist memorabilia captured and forced Blacks "into images they did not devise" suggests.

The result of this broad-based operation is an insidious falsifying ego that subjects and enslaves individuals both socially and culturally, forcing them to identify with the degraded state of being that they have internalized. Fanon dramatizes this situation in the following hypothetical, yet tragically real, situation:

> As I begin to recognize that the Negro is the symbol of sin, I catch myself hating the Negro. But then I recognize that I am a Negro. There are two ways out of this conflict. Either I ask others to pay no attention to my skin, or else I want them to be aware of it. I try then to find value for what is bad – since I have unthinkingly conceded that the black man is the color of evil. In order to terminate this neurotic situation, in which I am compelled to choose an unhealthy, conflictual solution, fed on fantasies, hostile, inhuman in short, I have only one solution: to rise above this absurd drama that others have staged round me, to reject the two terms that are equally unacceptable, and, through one human being, to reach out for the universal.[9]

While Fanon's solution is assuredly modernist in terms of its quest for universals and essences, Alice Walker's is incipiently postmodernist since she attempts to imaginatively project herself into the dimly lit world of the past in order to see how individuals might confront the stereotypes enslaving them. In contrast, Kara Walker's development is manifestly postmodernist, as we will see, since it views the world in terms of clichéd historical romances that reduce all humanity to stereotypes, which, by their own definition, are locked into the rigidities of limited perspectives.

In a lecture given to the School of the Arts, Virginia Commonwealth University, on October 24, 2000, Kara Walker alluded to the type of Lacanian reading of stereotypes that Fanon proposes. It is worth noting that her images have been so daunting that the Fanon connection has not been mentioned in the voluminous literature on her. "When stereotypes attempt to take control of their own bodies," Walker pointed out, referring to Blacks at large, "they can only do what they are made of, and they are made of the pathological attitudes of the Old South. Therefore, the racist stereotypes occurring in my art can only partake of psychotic activities." Rather than subscribing to the previous generation's crusade to create a morally uplifting and regenerative art capable of revivifying stereotypes, Walker's statement suggests that well-intended efforts by such artworks as Betye Saar's *The Liberation of Aunt Jemima*, 1972, are doomed to failure since even the most seemingly benign stereotype, by its very nature, has created in Walker's words an "unredeemable" form of alienation.[10] Regarding this entire generation's desire to gentrify images of Blacks, Walker succinctly commented, "I saw a lot of works steeped in history and in the awareness of self and pride—and enormous intangibles, issues that often get didactic."[11]

Over the past decade, Kara Walker has made a concerted study of blackface imagery. Since most of this material dates to the late nineteenth century when high-speed presses, new and better means of reproduction, cheaper paper, and increased literacy created a means of producing and distributing information to mass audiences, racist stereotypes developed under these conditions have provided

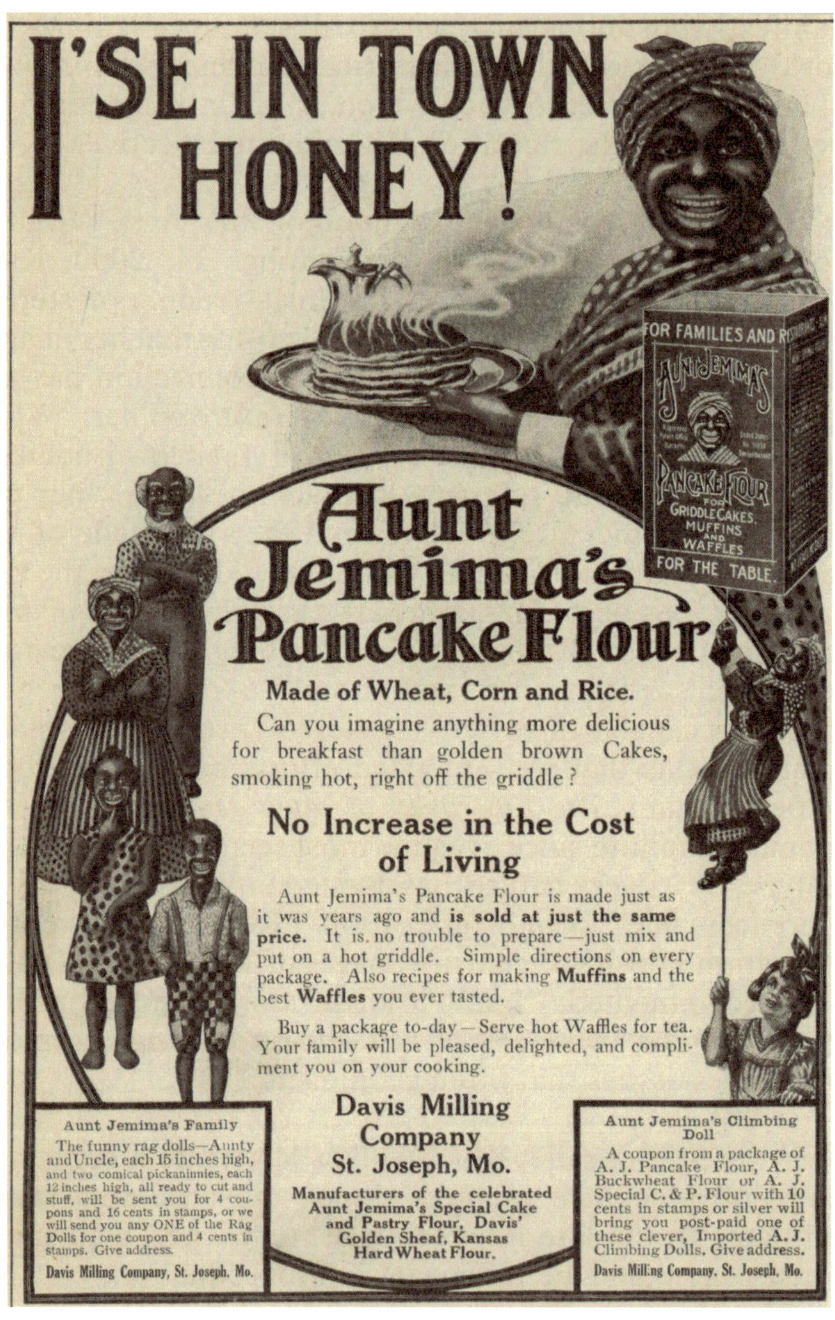


Aunt Jemima's Pancake Flour advertisement, *Ladies' Home Journal*, December 1, 1910. The Miriam and Ira D. Wallach Division of Art, Prints and Photographs: Picture Collection, The New York Public Library

revealing insights into mainstream popular opinion, which, at the time, was predominately white. In desperate need of compensating for the increased and highly suspect racist practices of the period, including unprecedented lynching, this newly developed popular-culture machinery helped to produce and disseminate public opinion by making "the Negro" the butt of a concerted "humor" campaign. This tacit yet widely held approach apparently relieved tensions in the white community at the same time that it reinforced the dominant belief that Blacks were members of an inferior race. No matter how despicable they might be, these images have proven useful to Walker since they guarantee her access to the broad historical effects of ideology that have constituted a cultural and racist collective unconscious.[12] This historical framework, predicated on the mass appeal of blackface memorabilia, together with the recent relevancy of this material in the ideological war now taking place, resonates with her art.

When she was still an undergraduate art student at the Atlanta College of Art, Walker, together with schoolmate Jennifer Cawley, would visit neighboring Stone Mountain Village gift shops, located in close proximity to the rock-carved Confederate Memorial, which honors the South's major heroes, with the express purpose of finding particularly offensive mass-produced pieces of racist collectibles.[13] The practice has continued intermittently over the years, and has resulted in Walker's filling one wall of her studio with such images. As she explained to curator Liz Armstrong:

> I keep at least one section of the wall filled with images of popular racism, Americana of the sort African American intellectuals find compelling as collector's items. Actually, several of the postcards and posters I keep are contemporary reproductions of nineteenth and early

> twentieth-century advertising images: some are authentic, and some are recent images that are reminiscent of an earlier brand of racism, a less self-conscious brand.[14]

While this part of the Armstrong interview establishes Walker's credentials as a collector of Black memorabilia, the next section provides insight into the slippery quagmire of signification in which she has willingly become enmeshed. Citing the example of a well-known photograph that adorns her studio wall, Walker wonders if one can in fact disembrace one's self from the imprisoning mirror image of the racist stereotype:

> Like an Annie Leibovitz postcard of Whoopi Goldberg (an avid collector of Afro-Americana, herself) immersed, spread-eagle, in a bathtub full of milk. It's obviously meant to be provocative, but pinned up next to an old card featuring a cartoon of a classically posed, nappy-headed nude black girl, intended as a parody of beauty, it's problematic.
>
> The reason I collect these images is really for their sheer strangeness, the almost open-endedness of meaning—you know, because racism is *so direct*, there's usually no difference between an insult and an end result. But, as an artist looking at what for better or worse is artwork, I sense the love/hate relationship these earlier artists must have had for their subject. Blacks, or in the case of these images, niggers, coons, pickanninies, mammies, and so on, are rendered not only as second-class and subhuman, but also as picturesque peasants. Every possible variation on the general theme *race* gets a place in my picture file, exoticism and creolization

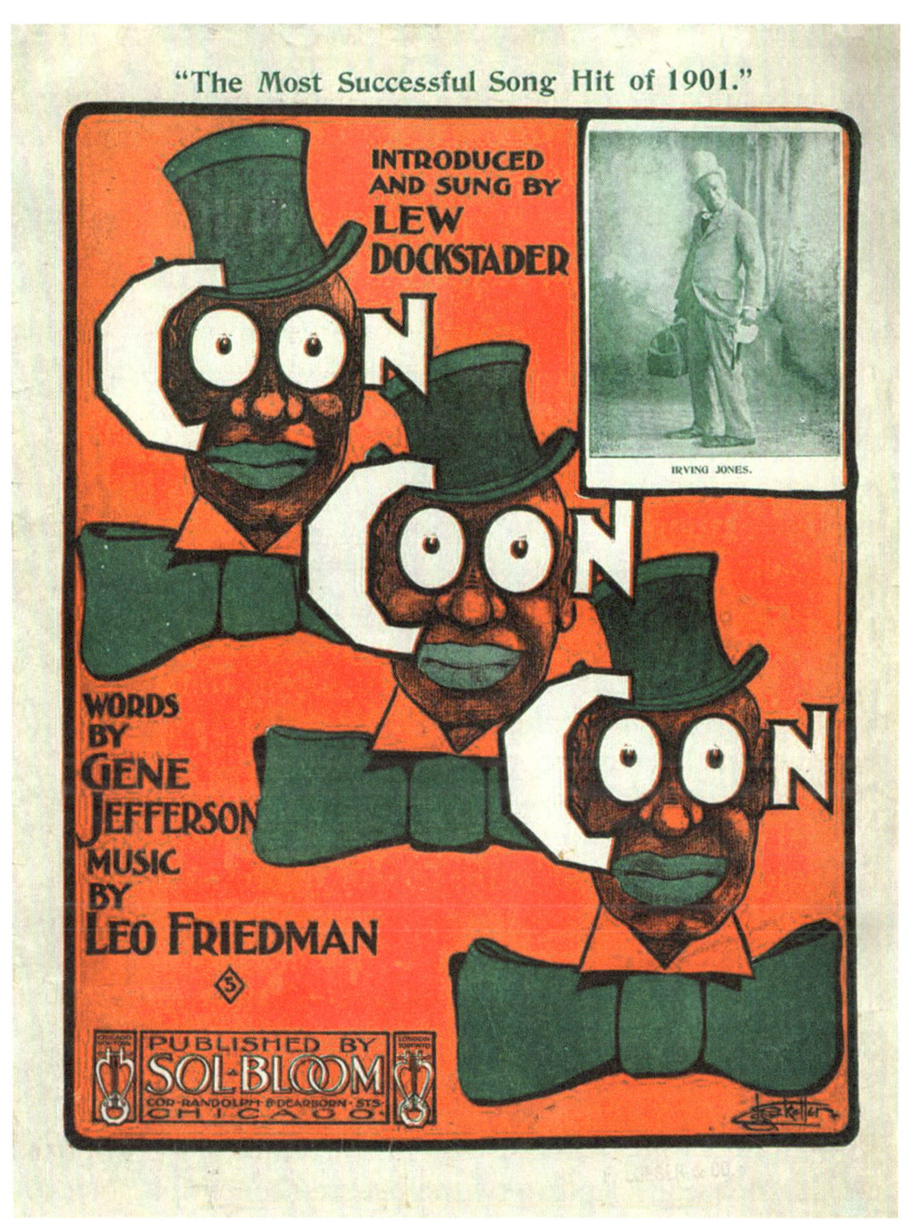


Sheet music for Gene Jefferson (words) and Leo Friedman (music), "Coon, Coon, Coon," 1901, Sol Bloom

and lust and romance and the Civil War and cinema and hate groups . . . these are all areas of interest.[15]

Walker's empathy for the white artists' making these images is commendable and also necessary for her art. Rather than pointing fingers at certain groups and taking refuge in a moral high ground that might elevate her work at the same time that it would isolate her, she prefers to create an art in which the well-oiled machinery of ensconced ideology begins to sputter, to start and stop intermittently, calling attention to itself and its creaky and outmoded terms. In the interim, it envelops, impugns, and implicates its audience's own history, as well as its creator's, generating in the process the uneasy realm that Walker refers to as "my inner plantation." In an important interview with critic Jerry Saltz, she elaborates:

> I guess that's what this generation of black kids is going to inherit. And this "inner plantation" is this grand place where, to some extent, we knew our place; a place where one is whole, in that sense, and knows what to fight against, or what not to fight against, or who to obey, or how to hold on to oneself in the face of oppression.[16]

We might also contemplate this "inner plantation" as the metaphoric projection of mainstream values on African American culture, resulting in the distorting realm of shadows known as racist stereotypes. The idea that Blackness is a racist construct projected onto the "Negro populace" by a dominant white society is a concept Fanon first proposed in his famous description of the primal scene of a "Negro" striking terror in a young white child, who projects on him the state of Blackness and evil, and thereby becomes the authority figure Fanon calls "the white man" in the following statement: “On that day, completely dislocated, unable to be abroad with the other, the white man, who unmercifully imprisoned me,” Fanon writes, “I took myself far off from my own presence, far indeed, and made myself an object. . . . My body was given back to me sprawled out, distorted, recolored, clad in mourning in that white winter day.”[17] In her art, Walker first literalizes this penumbral realm as black silhouettes and then disturbs them so that at times they assume the configuration of an orgy of interpenetrating bodies, thus subverting the binary oppositions on which Fanon’s work is predicated. As her panoramic frieze *Slavery! Slavery!* clearly demonstrates, slavery in both its historical and ideological phases is as insidious as it is incestuous. In her shadow plays, she purposely confuses the external metaphoric light sources that cause shadows so that they are cast not only from the vantage point of the dominant culture but also from the formerly subjected one, creating a strange and insane region worthy of Francisco Goya, who, in fact, made a remarkable small painting of an insane asylum.

Walker’s world, however, extends far beyond Goya’s in that the insanity she pictures is not a direct transcription of the external world but, instead, is the ossified and dehumanizing world of the stereotypical, similar to the art of Andy Warhol, which she has acknowledged admiring.[18] But Walker is more than a mere Warhol follower, she is in fact a fellow traveler since she has discovered her own terrain in the fictionalized histories constituting the contemporary genre of Harlequin Romance novels and their turn-of-the-twentieth-century antecedents. These cheap, pulp-fictionalized histories are the novelistic counterpart to the blackface contemptible collectibles that have unleashed the recent spate of ideological battles we have been discussing.

In order to discover the tremendous power of Harlequin Romance novels and their perpetuation of racist stereotypes,

Walker herself had to be subjected to the analogous situation of becoming someone else's stereotype. This painful and unprovoked experience occurred when she was still living in the South. It resulted in a need to construct a pseudonymous identity for herself as a stereotype, which is in turn capable of generating a new series of stereotypes. The situation is akin to having her shadow, her alias, give birth to a new order of being. Its distinct advantage is the distance it creates between herself and her imagery, allowing her to heighten the stereotypical nature of her imagery so that its removal from the real world is one of its key features. Instead of using herself as the lens for viewing the past, she enlists the aid of an alias from another time as the perspective on which to assess the contemporary world, so that the present is viewed in terms of the past. But this bygone era is an ideological past, not simply a distant historical period; in other words, it is the fictionalized version of the past that has developed according to the rigid genre rules of Harlequin Romance novels. Walker elaborated on the complexity of her situation in her interview with Armstrong:

> I'm trying to set up a narrative for myself that references . . . a fictional construct through which I tend to view much of my life. A fiction—I mean like a novel, with a heroine and an almost discernible plot. . . . And not just any old bad novel, but a very specific bad novel that is set in the South, with all of the dripping Spanish moss and illicit desires and politics and stuff that come with history and blackness. And all the problems that come up in interracial relationships—how walking with somebody white in the street would automatically trigger a response that was one hundred fifty years old, terms like "nigger lover" or "race traitor." It thrust me and the other person into a situation that we're thinking we had suppressed

> in the 1990s. [I thought] the thirty years or so between the Civil Rights Movement and where I am today had somehow wiped all of that out, you know, and we were all getting along and holding hands. So I grew up in this environment of loving and respecting the "other" and being very open to everyone and having that turn on me.[19]

Her pseudonym initially took on the wonderfully archaistic sobriquet "Miss K. Walker, A Free Negress of Noteworthy Talent," which was first used for *Gone*. The pseudonym was a hybrid predicated on the tensions that developed from her readings of such slave narratives as Harriet Jacobs's *Incidents in the Life of a Slave Girl* and such racist novels as Thomas Dixon Jr.'s *The Clansman*,[20] which served as the basis of D. W. Griffith's film *The Birth of a Nation* and spans the first years of Reconstruction from 1865 to 1870.[21] Then Walker incarcerates both types of narration in the genre strictures of the Harlequin Romance so that these earlier writings become the initial alembic that is then further distilled in terms of the distinct parameters used for contemporary pulp fiction. According to Dixon's story, Lydia Brown, the mulatto mistress of Austin Stoneman, is portrayed as dragging her white lover into her "black abyss of animalism." Walker remembers her as being characterized by Dixon as "tantalizing . . . with grotesquely large lips, whose dirty hair is tied with dirty ribbons; catlike."[22] Besides these sources, the persona of Miss K. Walker also draws on the artist's childhood fantasies about what life would be like if she had been born a slave, fantasies that no doubt were catalyzed by her move at age thirteen from a liberal community in Stockton, California, to the reactionary town of Stone Mountain, Georgia,[23] and that were motivated moreover by her early readings of historical romances similar to Barbara Ferry Johnson's *The Heirs of Love*, from which she excerpted the following in a brief piece for the magazine *Bomb*:

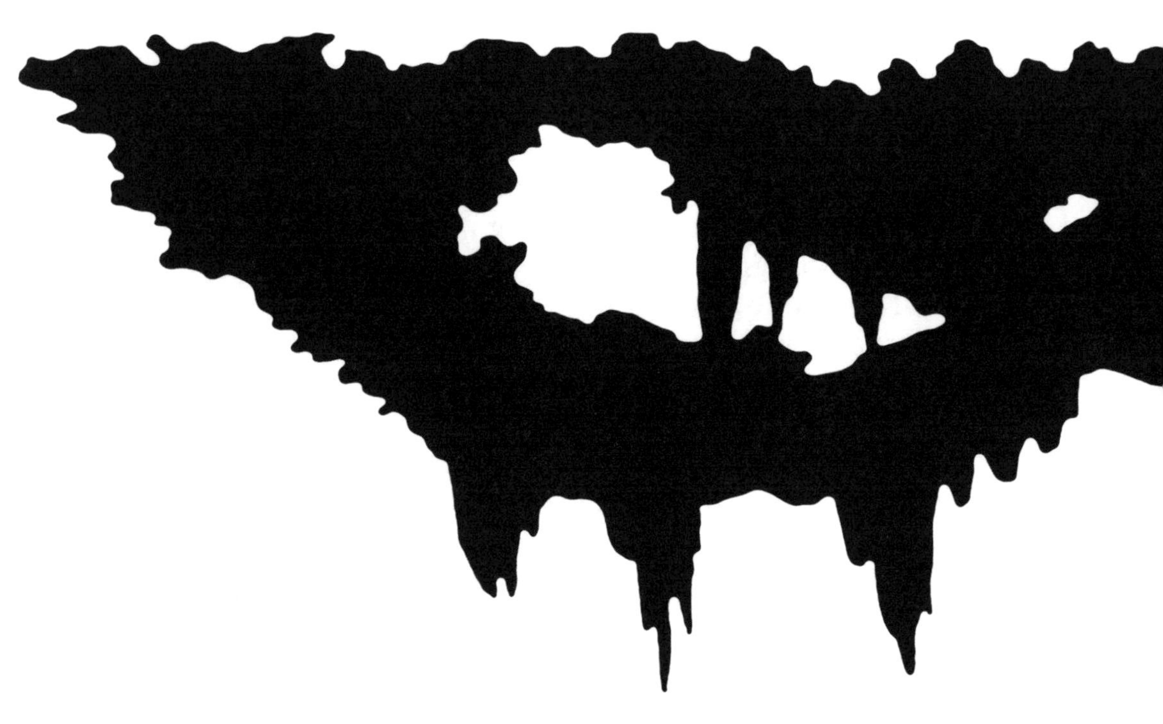

Kara Walker, *Slavery! Slavery!* (detail)

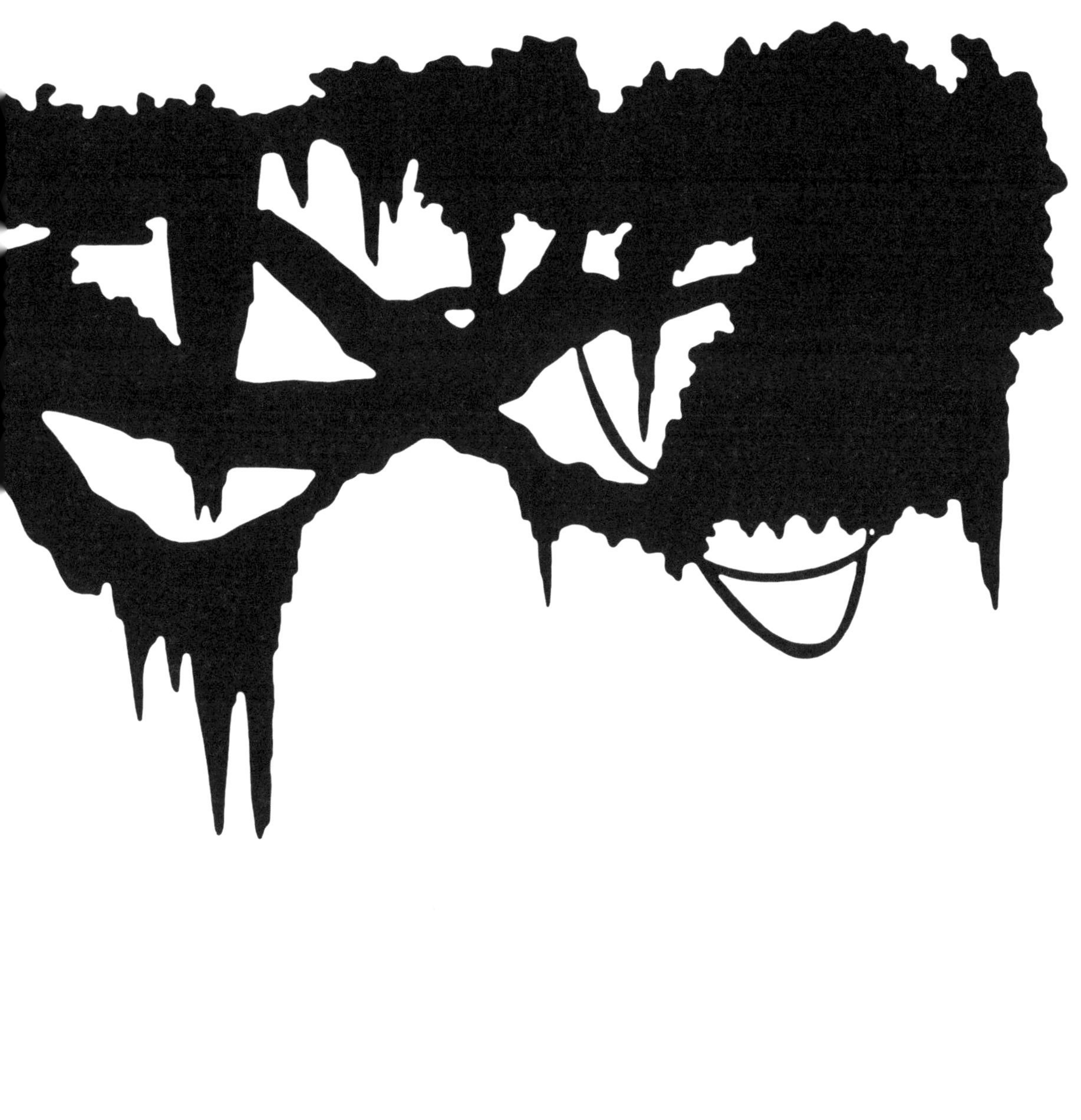

> She had always yearned to create a new identity for herself as the wife of a white man. . . . Why this yearning to return to a place that had harbored . . . the humiliation of being an octoroon in a white-dominated world?[24]

Responding to this excerpt, Walker commented, "Historical romances are the by-product of self-hatred, internalized sexism, and a remarkable kind of racism, the kind that makes one comfortable enough with it to become lustful for it," thus critiquing while indicating how one might be inadvertently implicated in such narratives.

This passage, together with Walker's commentary, helps to explain the basis for one of this artist's most controversial assessments: "All black people in America want to be slaves just a little bit." As she told Saltz, the rest of this statement included the sentence, "[Slavery] gives people heaping teaspoons of dignity and pride."[25] She went on to explain:

> I guess slavery is the ultimate oppression. To be a slave runs along the lines of being a better masochist and knowing how to put up with things. It's that strength that entitles you to brace yourself for—I don't know—finding that thing that helped your grandmother or great-grandmother get through it all; made her such a strong person. Without that sense of oppression, ironically, it seems difficult to progress.[26]

Although Walker implies how one might be implicated in such a contradictory and tradition-honored process of aggrandizement through debasement, her overall search is as much sociological and categorical as it is personal and idiosyncratic. These insights as well as her art indicate a need to discover the ideological mechanisms responsible for the social and historical construction of both Blacks and whites at the end of the twentieth century and the beginning of the twenty-first century. In her work she detonates these ideological mechanisms with sexual imagery, using the same tools with which the unconscious mind sometimes avails itself when it wishes to bring particular contents to consciousness, so that her pieces are as potentially shocking to her as they are to her viewers. As Walker explained to *New York Times* critic Julia Szabo, "I can understand it [the unsettling subject matter of my art], and I can't even really talk my way out of it. I can't say, 'Well, you shouldn't be offended.' Why not? It's a valid response, it's a valid way to feel."[27]

The same year that Walker created *Slavery! Slavery!*, she made a red, white, and blue sketch that played on the format of nineteenth-century theatrical broadsides used to advertise blackface minstrel shows. Complete with images of the US and Confederate flags, this drawing contains the following copy that wryly captures, with incisive and even bitter wit, the customary nineteenth-century "patriotic" style of hyperbolic fanfare with which the artist would no doubt like to introduce her cycloramic frieze. It reads:

1846 1996
Slavery
Slavery!
Presenting
As detail'd in the Fabulous
And
True-to-Life
Experiences
Of Yours Truly
Missus K.E.B. Walker
A Free Black Negress of Color
Who Possesses

A One Hundred and Fifty Years Vision of
The American South
And
Picturesque Slavery
Witness
This Daily Changing Shadow Show
The Grand "Moving" Romance
Of Our Time[28]

The feigned humor of this text, the exultant tone that a sideshow barker would use to hype the show, the backhanded compliment to the artist that redundantly emphasizes her status as "A Free Black Negress of Color," and the dynamics of a shadow theater purporting to present 150 years of the dynamics of slavery that she characterizes as "The Grand 'Moving' Romance Of Our Time" all reveal the layers of irony making up this work. But as rife with period satire as this piece is, it does not prepare viewers for the extraordinary effect achieved by the 85-foot-long cyclorama, *Slavery! Slavery!*

The full title of this 1997 piece, which was expressly made for Richard Flood's Walker Art Center exhibition *No Place (Like Home)*, also reads like a piece of nineteenth-century theatrical flummery. With its idiosyncratic style of capitalization recalling nineteenth-century populist forms of advertising and their often rudimentarily educated typesetters, it takes the following form: *Slavery! Slavery! Presenting a GRAND and LIFELIKE Panoramic Journey into Picturesque Southern Slavery or "Life at 'Ol' Virginny's Hole' (sketches from Plantation Life)" See the Peculiar Institution as never before! All cut from black paper by the able hand of Kara Elizabeth Walker, an Emancipated Negress and leader in her Cause.* The artist has revealed two sources for this piece. The first is the cyclorama depicting the Civil War–era Battle of Atlanta, which is the focus for the small yet well-known museum that houses it in this same city. A turn-of-the-twentieth-century, completely circular painted backdrop, this populist mural, which Walker characterizes as "history painting gone nuts—almost noble and ridiculous"[29] currently consists of a 358-foot-round by 42-foot-tall canvas that is segued into a full-fledged diorama by the three-dimensional staffage and its attendant stage set.[30]

In place of a battle scene, Walker has inscribed on the somewhat reduced format of her shadow theater in the round a version of Eastman Johnson's *Negro Life at the South* (also known as *Old Kentucky Home*), which was made in 1859, before the outbreak of the Civil War. The received wisdom regarding this painting is found in Wayne Craven's brief summary, contained in his textbook *American Art: History and Culture*, which underscores the ideological import of this work. According to Craven, the basic information regarding this painting is as follows:

> Although Johnson settled in Washington, his début was at the National Academy of Design in New York in 1859. There he exhibited *Old Kentucky Home or Life in the South* as it has come to be called. The picture, which reportedly represents a scene behind Johnson's father's house in Washington, won him instant recognition. The masterful, detailed execution of the painting reflects his Düsseldorf training, and it was praised for its accuracy and truthfulness. This was no abolitionist attack upon the issue of slavery, but a genre scene rich in homey vignettes of courting lovers, dancing children, and the melodious strumming of the banjo player.[31]

Craven's argument that the painting is truthful and not polemical, i.e., abolitionist, attests to the strengths of

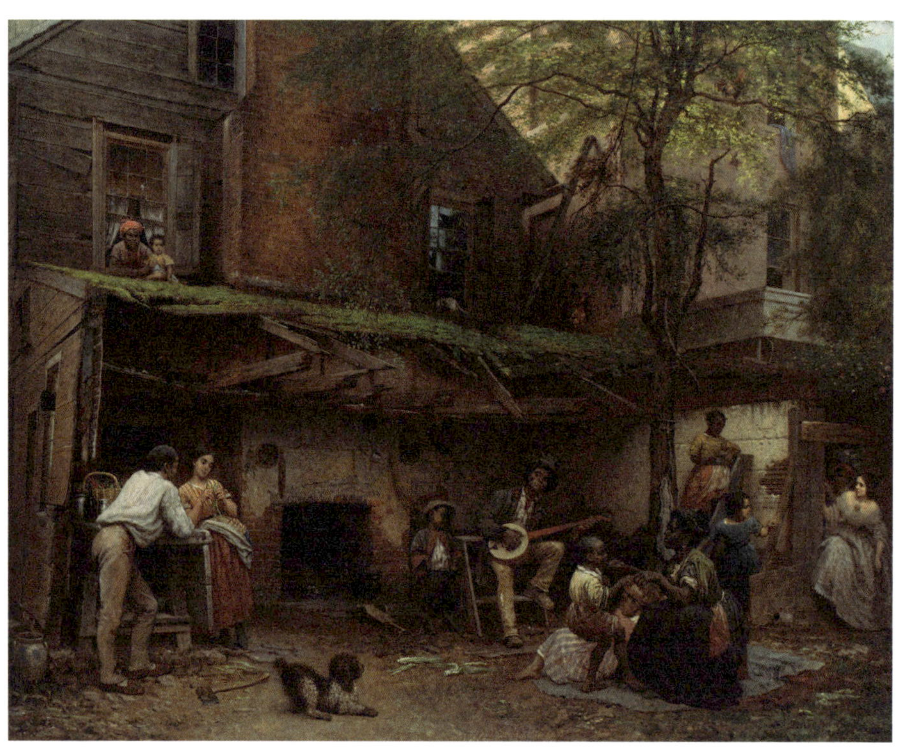

Eastman Johnson, *Negro Life at the South* (also known as *Old Kentucky Home*), 1859, oil on canvas, 37 × 46 inches (94 × 116.8 cm). The Robert L. Stuart Collection, the gift of his widow Mrs. Mary Stuart, S-225, New-York Historical Society. Photo: © New-York Historical Society

ideology during this time that subsequently have so thoroughly imbued our understanding of antebellum genre painting that their subjects are taken as direct transcriptions of reality rather than as social, cultural, and historical constructions that purport to reveal it. Such seamless ideologies are prized grist for Walker's deconstructive mill. Although Walker attests that her reading of Johnson's painting in *Slavery! Slavery!* is so personal that it is pointless for her to share her references,[32] a cursory look at the two works reveals a common interest in depicting whites and Blacks in an antebellum setting. In addition, since Johnson's title has over time become associated with the famous Stephen Foster song "My Old Kentucky Home," and thereby indirectly alludes to the minstrel shows for which this musician wrote some of his most important music, it can be considered the quintessential antebellum ideological norm against which Kara Walker takes literal umbrage. Although the motifs of the roof, the Black "granny" dancing with her child, and the entry of the young white mistress remain in Walker's version, most other elements in her frieze do not conform to Johnson's norm.

Before making such an imposing cyclorama as *Slavery! Slavery!*—and Walker has made twenty such monumental friezes in the past seven years—she customarily begins the actual creation of each cycle with only a brief set of notes regarding the identities of the figures, together with a number of summary thumbnail sketches. Her usual two-thirds life-size figures are then made on location. To begin the extraordinary on-site mental gymnastics involved in realizing such a work, Walker starts with long rolls of black photographer's backdrop paper taped to the wall. She roughly estimates the scale and position of her figures by summarily outlining them in white chalk. Then the paper is removed from the wall. Working on the floor, Walker incisively "draws" the figures with an X-Acto knife, removing them from their background in the process. At this point the figures have been conceived, drawn, and cut in reverse. Remaining still in this position, they are waxed before being flipped over and installed according to the artist's original concept.[33]

In an email to the author, Walker elaborated upon the complex iconography of *Slavery! Slavery!* The full enumeration of her letter is important not only for the information it provides about this specific cyclorama, but also because it demonstrates the way in which the artist invents her narrative prior to conceiving one of her monumental cycles. Walker writes:

> I generally begin "reading" *Slavery! Slavery!* from the central moon and then move out in both directions. This is the way I constructed it initially (actually it was moon, fountain, house, three points on the Walker compass).
>
> Beginning under the crescent moon, a woman vomits. I think of her as more African than slave, although her offspring behind her is beginning to resemble a peculiarly American sort of pickaninny. On her immediate left a white girl and boy scoop up bucketsful of slave's issue, toss it into the receiving boat—a false and impractical boat—tied to a dreamer, with holes for the legs. This boy/girl dreamer thinks of freedom.
>
> To the right of the vomiting woman, the mistress inspects a "Topsy-Turvy" doll and finds, instead of heads—one black and one white—only bottoms and legs. There is a little big house. Beyond it is a European-styled sambo in Turkish garb who sprays perfume under the skirts of a white

woman, whose proximity to blackness (especially in paintings) signifies her position as a prostitute. Her black mask confirms this. . . .

Next to her, a white man—something of a "Nigger lover"—bows at the feet of an all-giving black girl fountain. He farts his pleasure. Puffs of perfume and gas resemble speech bubbles.

The base of the "fountain of you" has a skull and a monkey. The fountain offers milk, blood, piss, spit or vomit. "Coffee, tea or me?" Or from childhood water fountain games: "Coffee, tea, milkshake, pee?"

The slave market consists of a trader who has a small cigar and a particular interest in making larger ones. The master threatens the young master-bater [*sic*] with "How it feels." (The hand is gunshaped to the mouth.)

Back to the moon in the center and moving to the left beyond the boat of the dreamer is a scene lifted lightly from Eastman Johnson's *Old Kentucky Home, or The Slave Quarter*, beginning with two white ladies of the big house trying to unlock the gate to the quarter. A vulnerable black stands with his backside against the keyhole. On the edge of the rooftop is an interracial coupling. There is a too-young soldier boy. A watermelon is hatching. Granny dances with a small child and is prepared to take the child out of this charade. A voodoo dancer and drummer replace the banjo player from the Eastman Johnson painting. A chicken appears with its head cut off, and a cut-off head replaces the one that is missing.

> The next scene is the underground railroad. Uncle Tom readies the family for escape. The pitchfork punctures the son. The girl child, eating an apple with her baby on her back, casually carts off the hay toward town and does not notice the pile of dung ahead or the KKK eyes in the North Star above.[34]

Throughout this surreal enumeration of activities and characters composing *Slavery! Slavery!* in which whites and Blacks alike are encumbered by the night scene, making them both slaves of darkness and captives of their shadowy/stereotypical selves, Walker lists situations in which the permeability of the body is foregrounded: a Black woman vomits; a white man farts; the "fountain of you" offers milk, blood, piss, spit, or vomit; and a pile of dung lies ahead of the young girl eating an apple. Both the frequency of these occurrences and their heightened visceral effect indicate their overall importance to this piece. Taken together, they demand some form of resolution, and the one that is most clearly being alluded to is Julia Kristeva's notable study of the necessary self-rejection (abjection) that comes before Lacan's mirror stage. Her study took the form of *Powers of Horror: An Essay on Abjection*. Although this book proved in the 1980s to be crucial to the art of Mike Kelley, Andres Serrano, and Kiki Smith, only one reference in the literature on Kara Walker mentions it, even though critics have been quick to recite the litany of transgressions occurring in her work, which include, among others: rape, sodomy, fellatio, miscegenation, incest, and child molestation. Writing in *Grand Street*, critic Anne Doran notes in passing, "In Walker's spirited response to abject art, it is no longer clear who has the upper hand. Her technique is a leveling device through which everyone becomes black: both kin and non-kin, each one the disguised, mysterious 'other.'"[35]

We might note that Doran's reference is not to abjection per se but to abject art, which she implies is already passé, a 1980s phenomenon. But just as Lacan's well-known theory of the mirror stage can be productively rethought in terms of stereotypes, so can Kristeva's theory of abjection be reworked in terms of the dynamics of Blacks' ongoing definition of the self. Doran's reference, then, leaves us with a series of questions demanding answers. Among them: Why does Walker seed her work so plentifully with references to abjection? How does she use racist stereotypes to rethink abjection? And what is the relationship between abjection and slavery?

These questions may be best answered by referring again to Lacan's mirror stage as a type of slavery in which the self is encumbered by an external falsifying ego, which can be viewed on the cultural level as a stereotype. As defined by Kristeva, the abject is the unbearable state of liminality, which confuses, agitates, or incapacitates stable identities. It begins before the mirror stage when the child reacts against the mother who has been identified as part of the child's self and "ab-jects" her, and it continues throughout life as a means for throwing off one's current subjectivity prior to embracing some other object as one's identifying ego. As a literary theorist as well as a practicing psychoanalyst and philosopher, Kristeva views this condition in terms of the intrusions into the symbolic realm caused by the ongoing semiosis of language and subjectivity. We might fruitfully use this theoretical definition as a means for looking at abjection both socially and culturally as opposed to personally, and consider it in terms of the limiting sense of selfhood that racist stereotypes permit.

In relation to Walker's art we might think of abjection as a blurring of boundaries between self and shadow, Black and white, publicly sanctioned acts and transgressive ones,



*continued on page 66*

I generally begin "reading" *Slavery! Slavery!* from the central moon and then move out in both directions. This is the way I constructed it initially (actually it was moon, fountain, house, three points on the Walker compass).

Pages 50–65: Kara Walker, *Slavery! Slavery!* (details), accompanied by Walker's descriptions

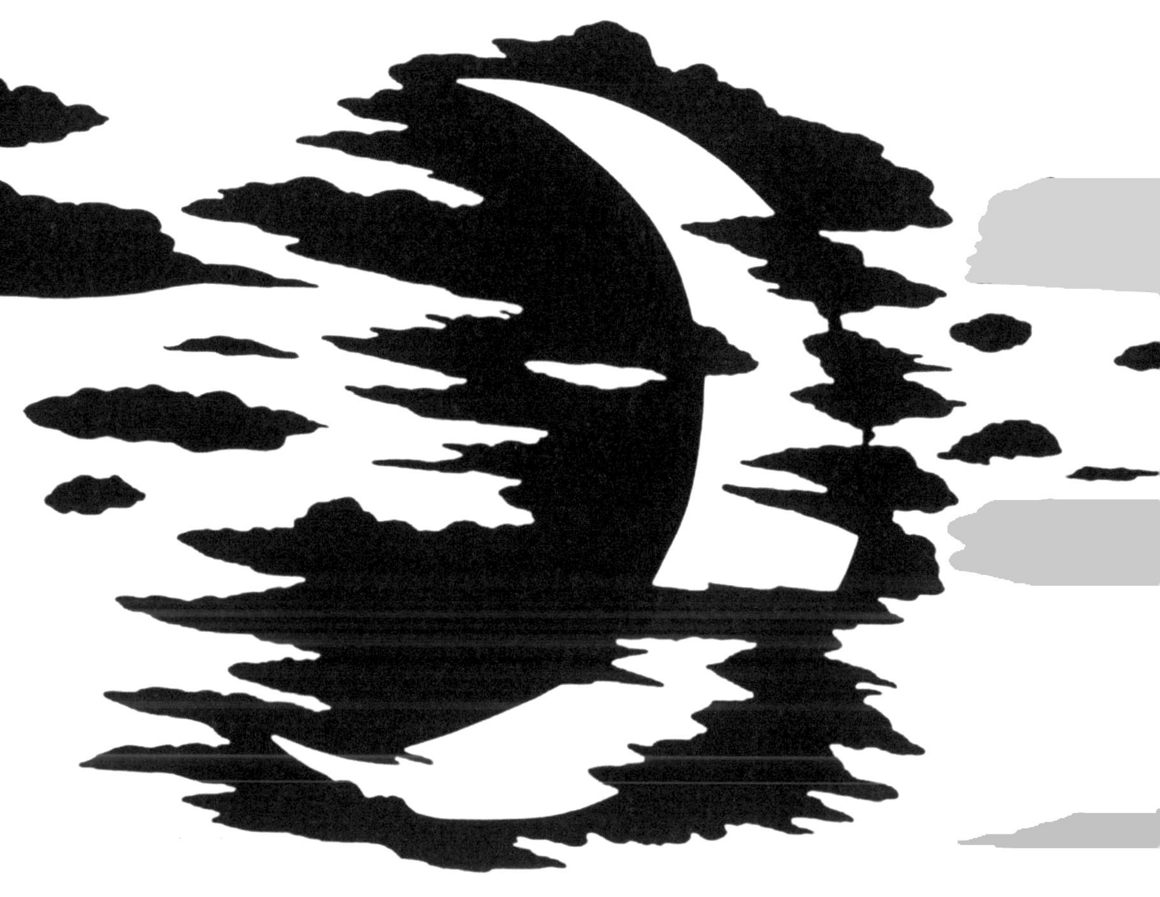

Beginning under the crescent moon, a woman vomits. I think of her as more African than slave, although her offspring behind her is beginning to resemble a peculiarly American sort of pickaninny.

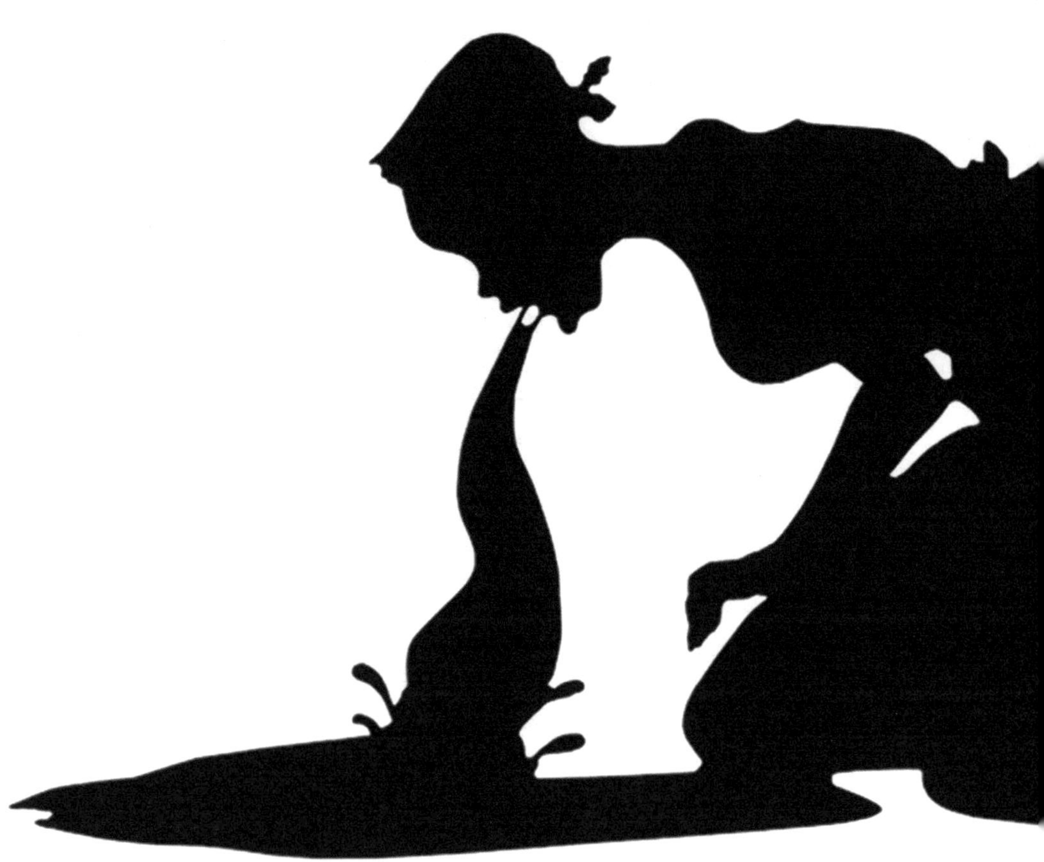

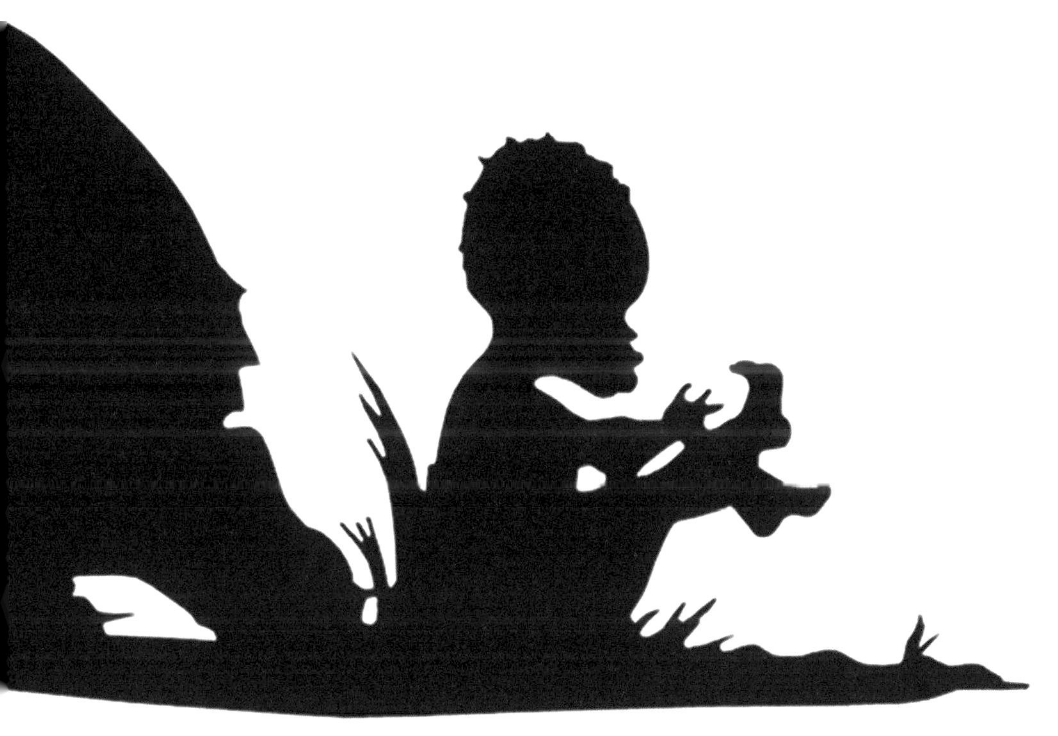

To the right of the vomiting woman, the mistress inspects a "Topsy-Turvy" doll and finds, instead of heads—one black and one white—only bottoms and legs.

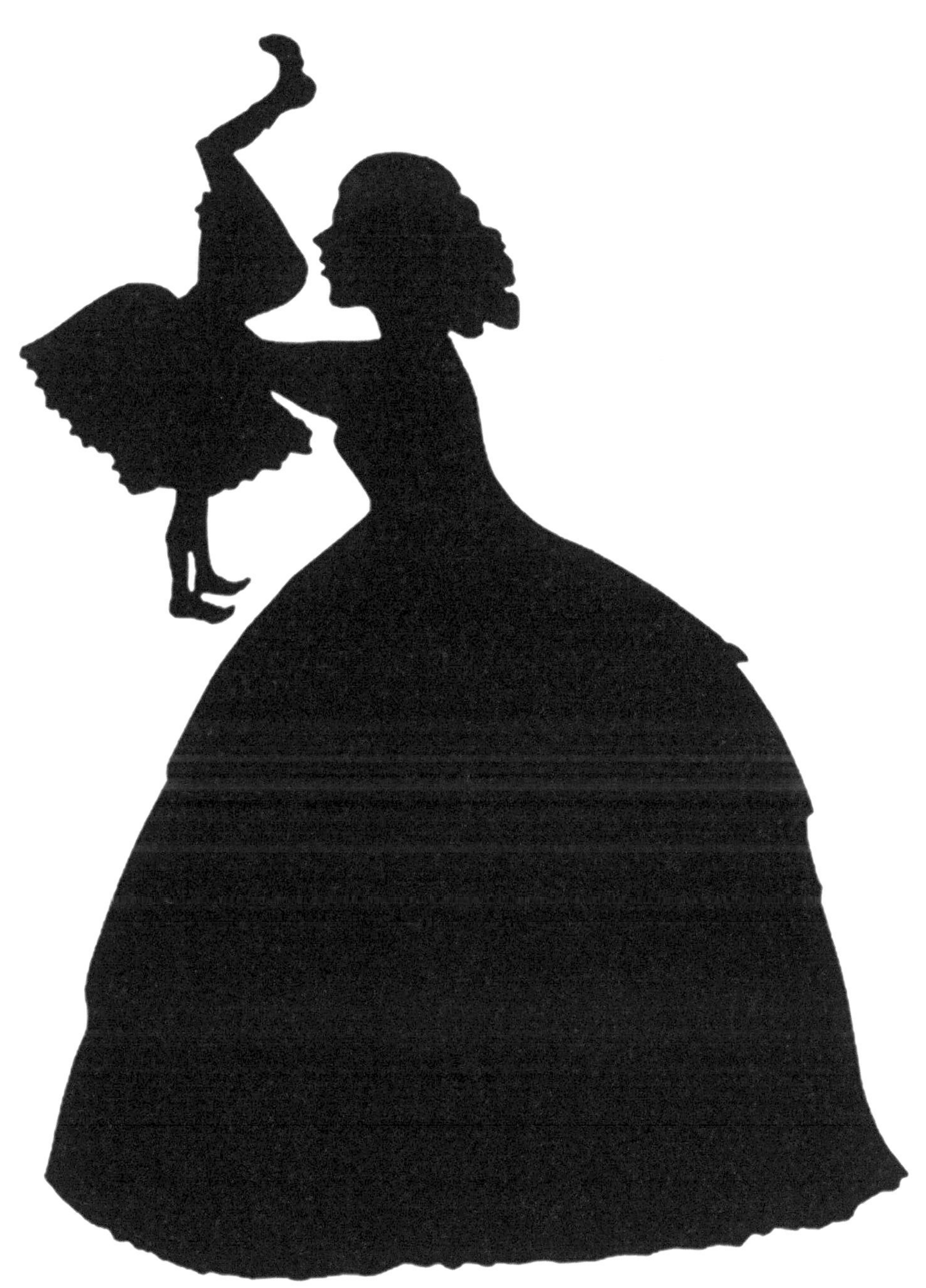

Beyond [the little big house] is a European-styled sambo in Turkish garb who sprays perfume under the skirts of a white woman, whose proximity to blackness (especially in paintings) signifies her position as a prostitute. Her black mask confirms this. . . .

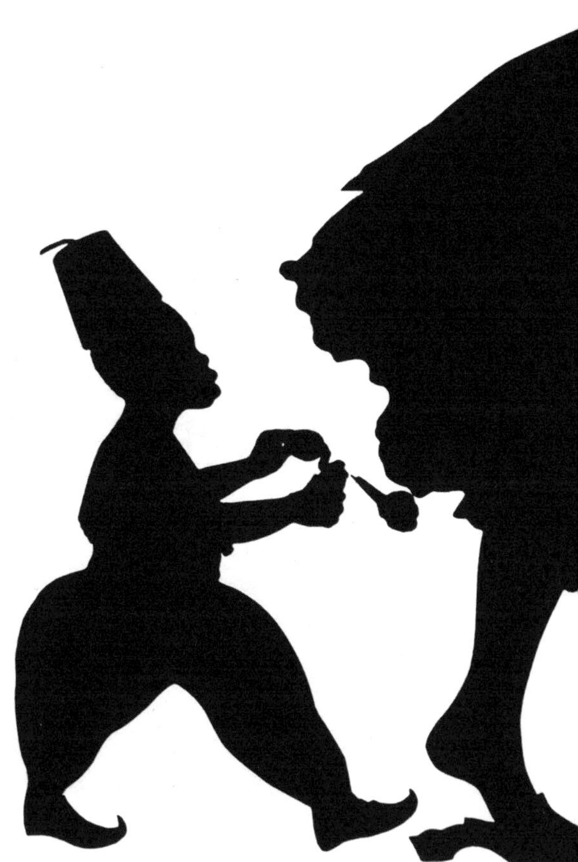

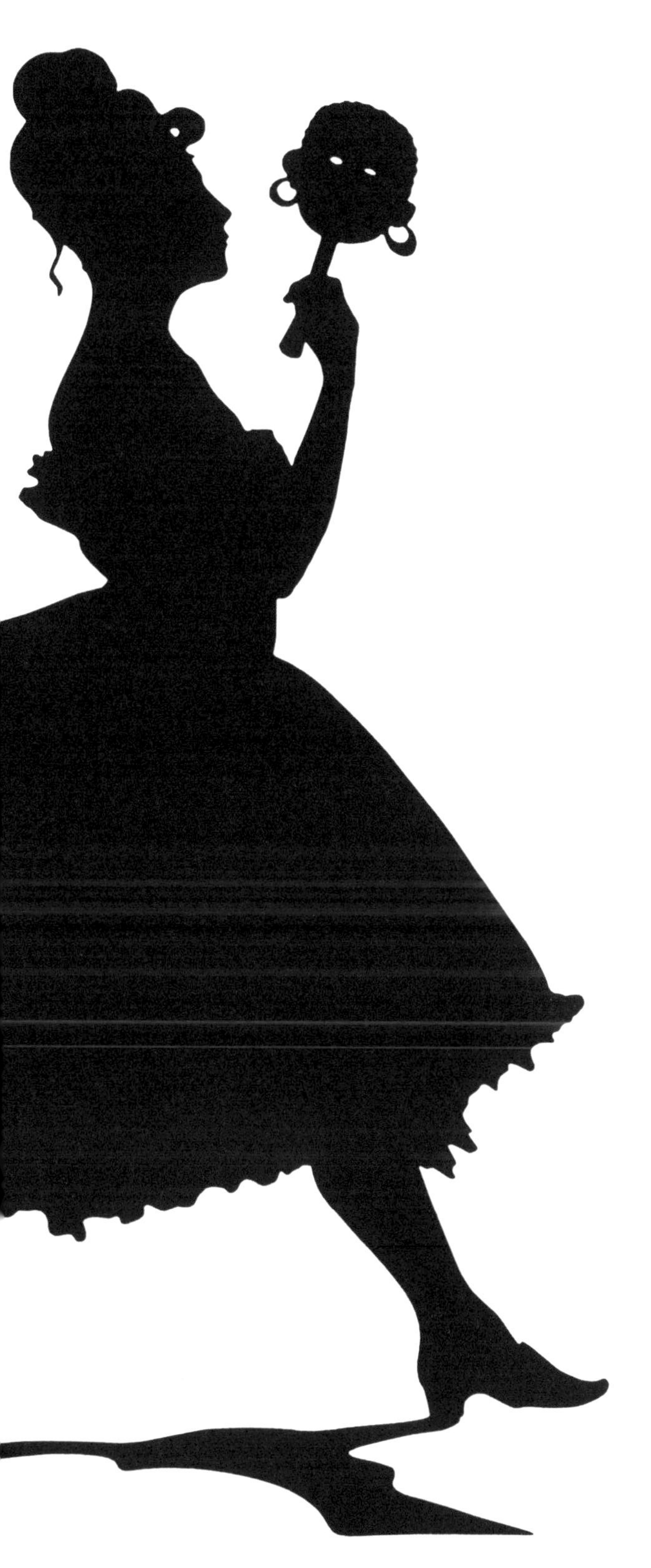

Next to her, a white man—something of a “Nigger lover”—bows at the feet of an all-giving black girl fountain. He farts his pleasure. Puffs of perfume and gas resemble speech bubbles.

The base of the “fountain of you” has a skull and a monkey. The fountain offers milk, blood, piss, spit or vomit. “Coffee, tea or me?” Or from childhood water fountain games: “Coffee, tea, milkshake, pee?”

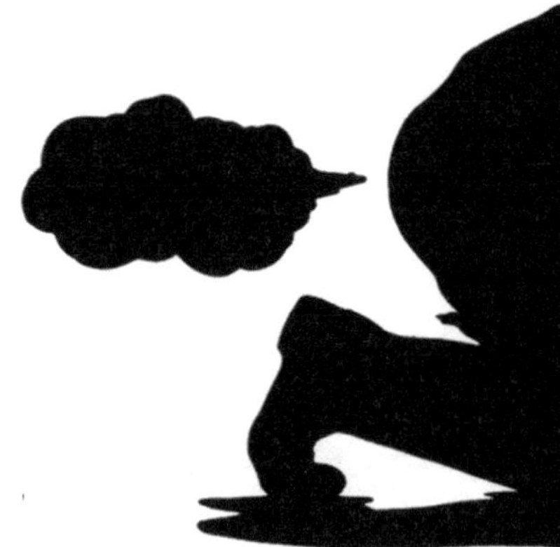

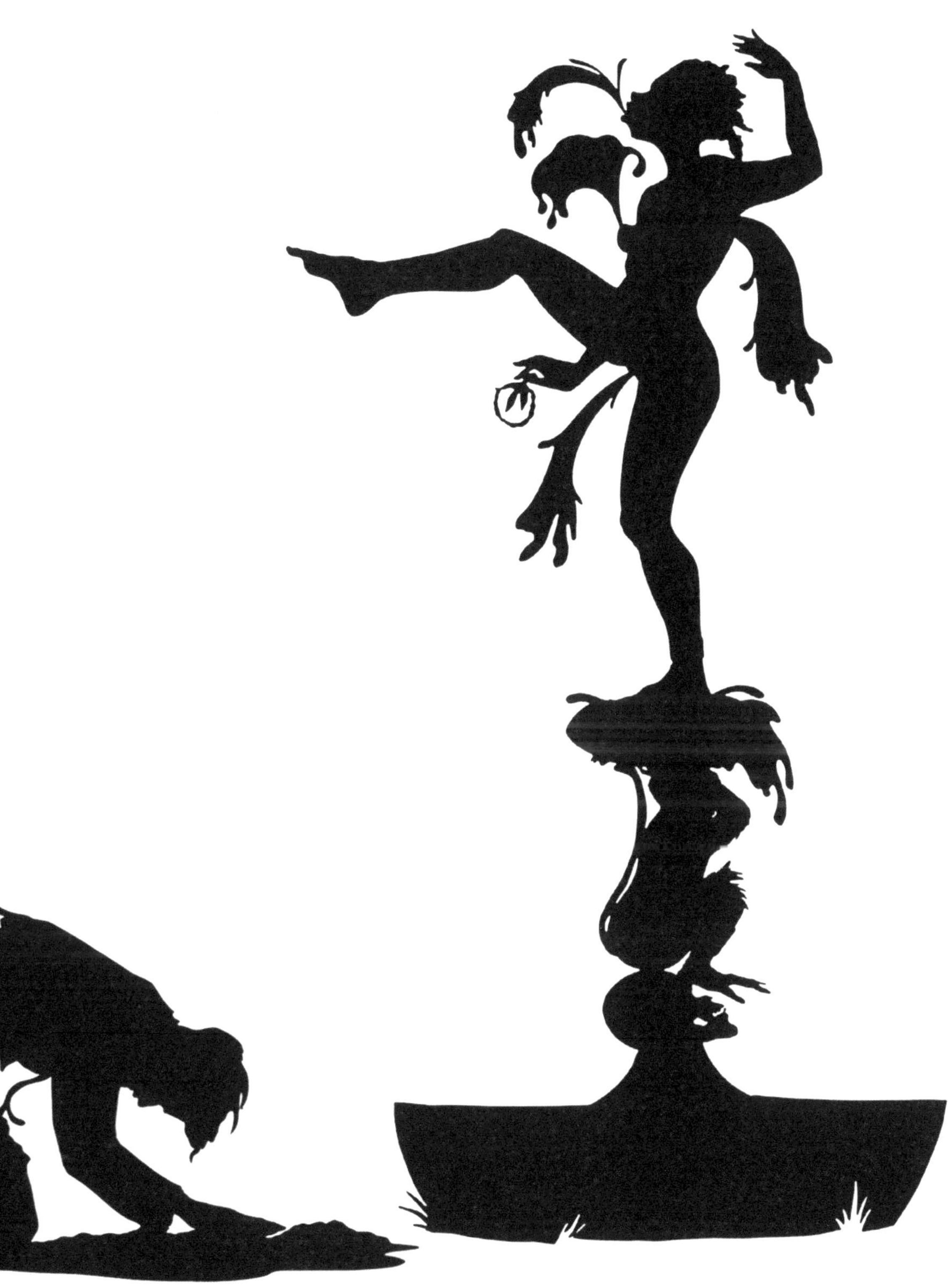

On the edge of the rooftop is an interracial coupling. There is a too-young soldier boy.

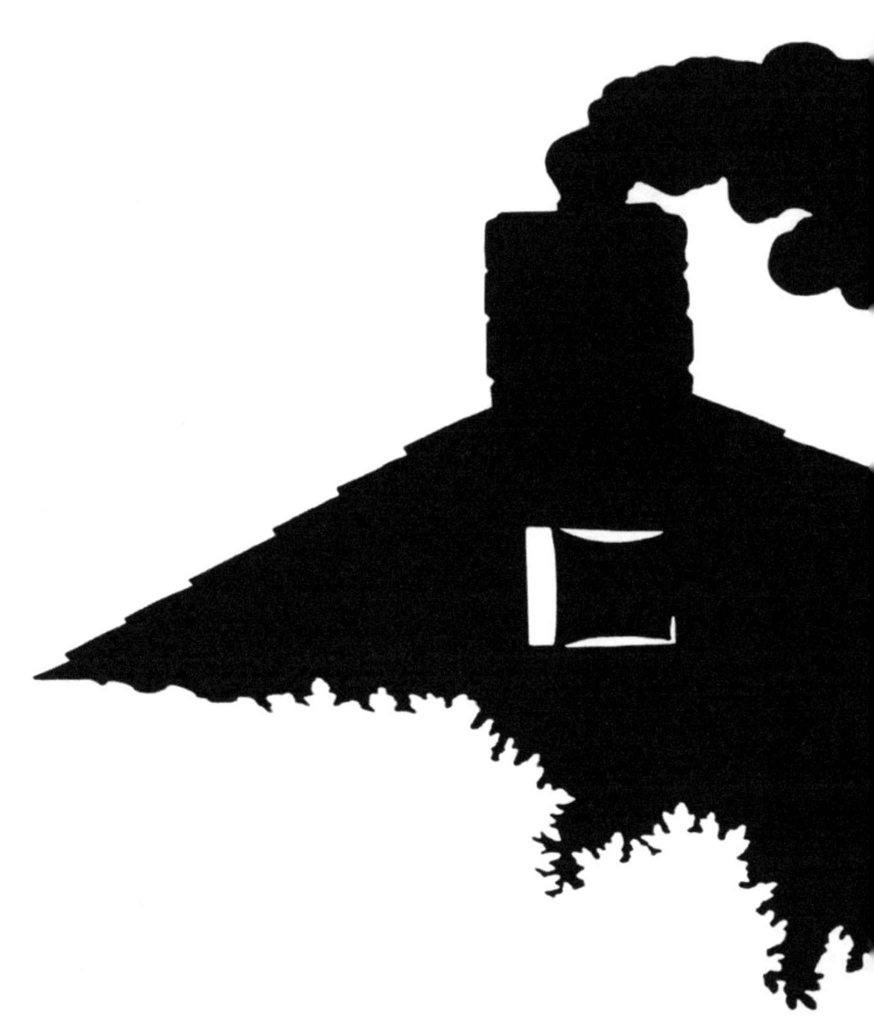

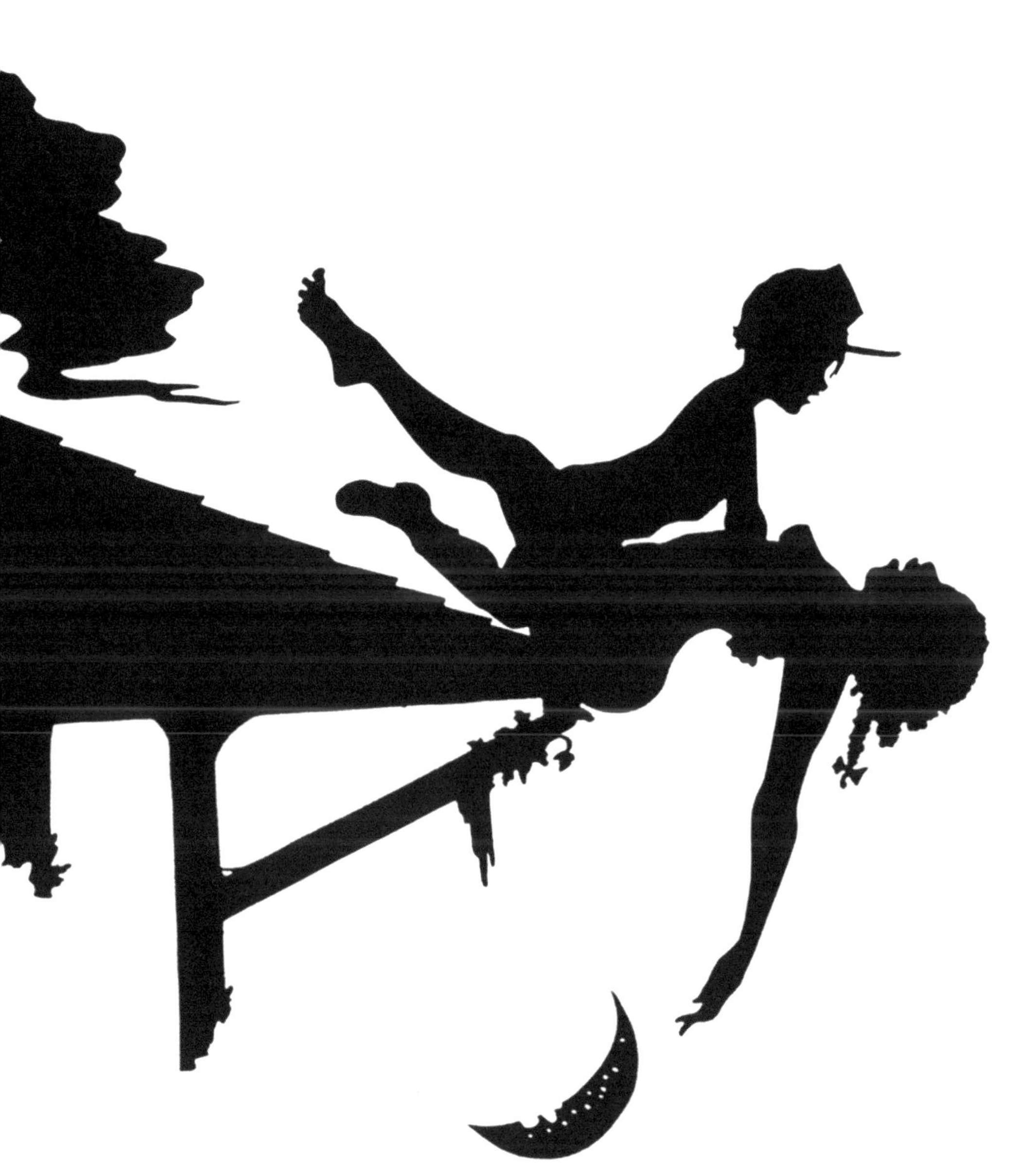

A watermelon is hatching. Granny dances with a small child and is prepared to take the child out of this charade. A voodoo dancer and drummer replace the banjo player from the Eastman Johnson painting. A chicken appears with its head cut off, and a cut-off head replaces the one that is missing.

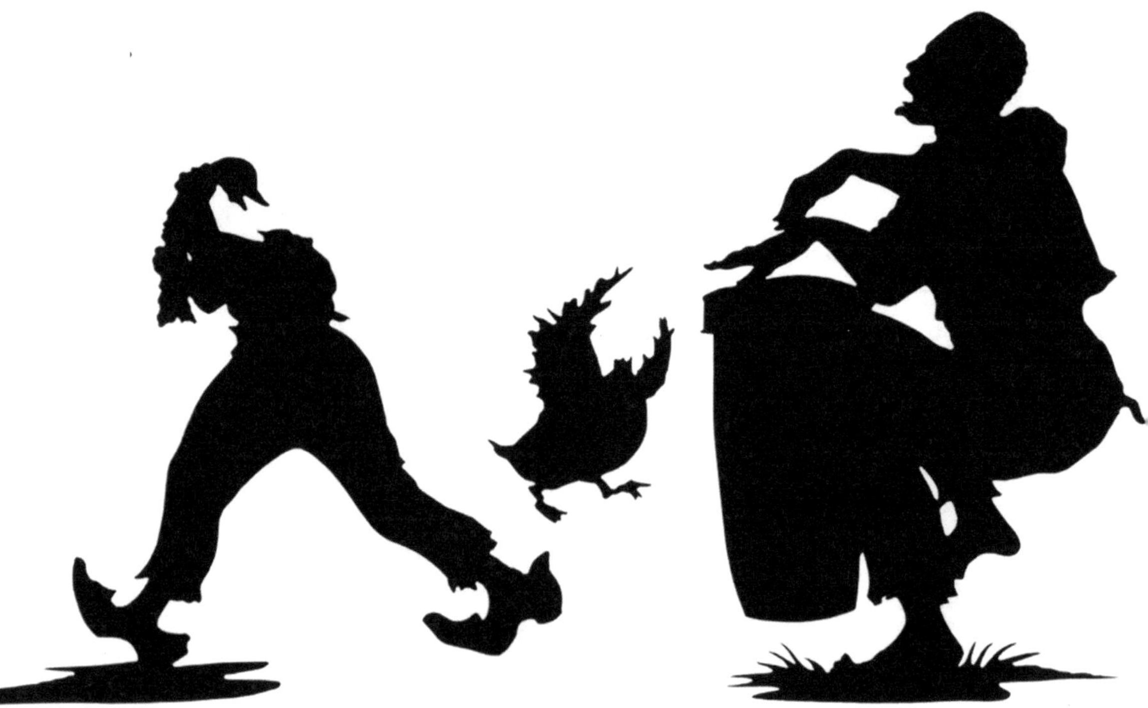

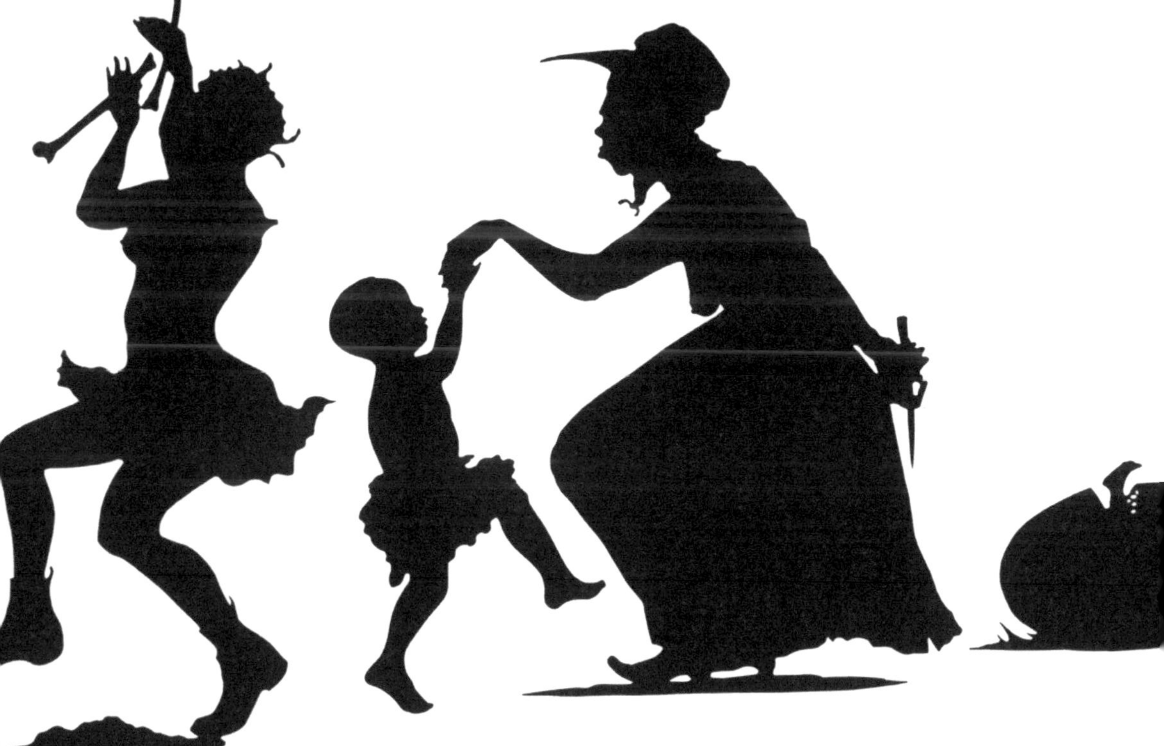

The girl child, eating an apple with her baby on her back, casually carts off the hay toward town and does not notice the pile of dung ahead or the KKK eyes in the North Star above.

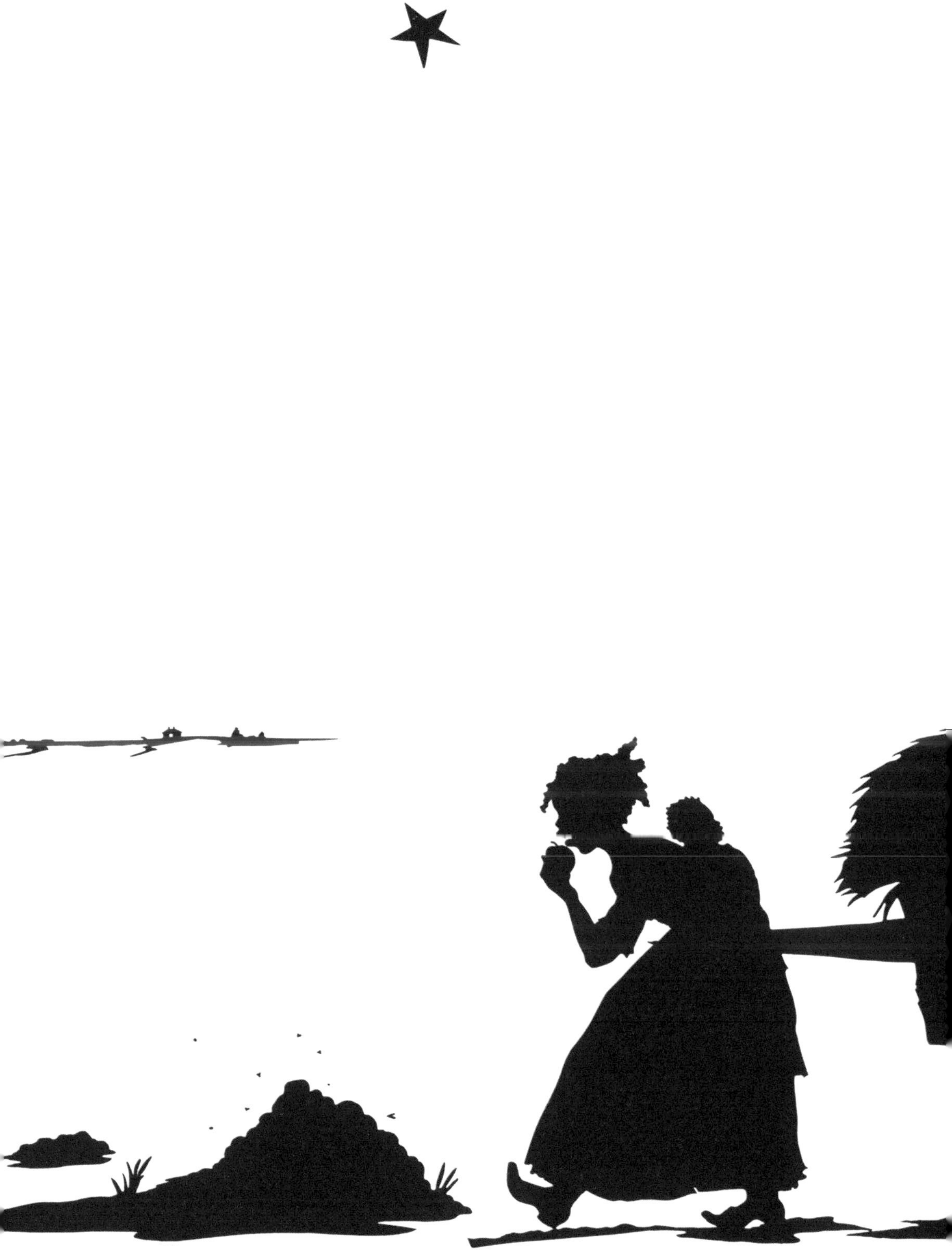

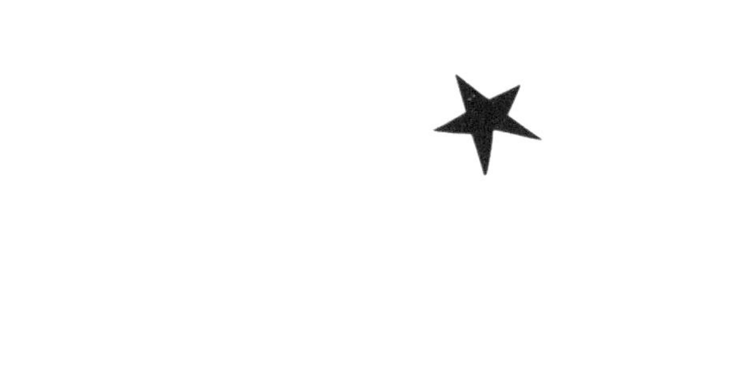

a new permeability that is capable of destroying established and limited subjectivities and opening the body of the social order, however briefly, to a more permeable world that experiences flows from the inside as well as from the outside. The ensuing destabilized abject realm becomes a virtual Garden of Delights on a par with Hieronymus Bosch's, in which couplings are less intended to constitute straightforward descriptions of orgiastic sex—although shock value does play an important role in characterizing the miasma of abjection—and more symbolic references to the obfuscation that results from undermining the established order of clearly defined stereotypes. The irony of Walker's work is her need to enter the stereotypical realm of the antebellum in order to combat it. And it should be pointed out that her antebellum world is constituted as much by the inherited views of Margaret Mitchell's *Gone with the Wind* and its many debasements comprising the narrative schemes of Harlequin Romance novels as it is a recapitulation and critique of Eastman Johnson's own highly ideological assumptions regarding slavery's naturalness. Conceptualized as the sense of emptiness that comes before the formation of a new ego—the void into which the present definition of the self is given up with no thought or hope of a new unifying ego—abjection represents the midnight of existence that Walker portrays as an insubstantial domain of vacancy lying beneath the surface of stereotypes. This sense of hollowness may be one of the reasons why Walker referred to the young, pretty Black girl in her series of early drawings, catalyzed by her reading of the 1984 racist pornographic novel *The Master's Revenge* (from the *Slave Horrors* series, published by Star Distributors), which pictures life on an antebellum plantation, as "a black hole, a space defined by the things sucked into her . . . a complication . . . [who] is simultaneously sub-human and super-human,"[36] and also the hope for the future, because her condition is so dismal, so totally and unrelievedly abject.

In Walker's art, the equivalent to the black hole and abjection are the piles of dung, which she at first excuses as a sign for "letting it all hang out." Then she goes on to qualify feces as a metaphor for "finding one's voice in the wrong end; searching for one's voice and having it come out the wrong way."[37] The difficulty facing those who have been deemed stereotypical and have internalized even a smidgen of its pernicious effects is that their voices have already been co-opted and lost. According to Kristeva, "Excrement and its equivalents . . . stand for the danger to identity that comes from without: the ego threatened by the non-ego, society threatened by its outside, life by death. . . . Fecal matter signifies, as it were, what never ceases to separate from a body in a state of permanent loss in order to become *autonomous, distinct* from the mixtures, alterations, and decay that run through it."[38] In Walker's work, piles of dung are akin to the indistinct shadows that Plato's proverbial prisoners in the cave are forced to accept as real, signs that are as chimerical as the other shadows/stereotypes that populate the rest of Walker's penumbral frieze. Even though these shadows/stereotypes are as unreal as the external objects giving rise to egos in Lacan's mirror stage, their power resides in their fictiveness. In *Slavery! Slavery!* Walker contrasts the heap of excrement with the all-giving fountain. Both are two-dimensional paper stereotypes, but while the feces reinforces the emptiness of a self that has already evacuated (or, per Kristeva, "ab-jected") itself, the fountain celebrates an ongoing permeable and continuously fecund mirror image that holds out the promise of a fuller self image even though it is in essence just another stereotype. We might say that the dung and the fountain connote two different aspects of abjection: the dung signifies the hollowness that attends the rejection of one's current subjectivity, and the fountain portends a fuller, richer, and more complete self. Located on either side of the central moon in *Slavery! Slavery!*, the two represent different cycles in the anxious night of destabilization that is the condition of the abject state.

We might conclude that Walker's "fountain of you," worshipped by the kneeling white man, revels in the type of jouissance that Roland Barthes in *The Pleasure of the Text* describes as a transgressive "erotics and politics of reading"[39] and that Kristeva characterizes as the state "where the object of desire, known as object a [in Lacan's terminology], bursts with the shattered mirror where the ego gives up its image in order to contemplate itself in the Other."[40] Apropos this fountain, we might consider Walker's statement of a year earlier:

> I didn't want a completely passive viewer. Art means too much to me. . . . I wanted to make work where the viewer wouldn't walk away; he would either giggle nervously, get pulled into history, into fiction, into something totally demeaning and possibly very beautiful. . . . I wanted to create something that looks like you. It looks like a cartoon character, it's a shadow, it's a piece of paper, but it's out of scale. It refers to your shadow, to some extent to purity, to the mirror.[41]

After looking at how *Slavery! Slavery!* thematizes abjection in terms of less and more desirable stereotypes, which both Lacan and Kristeva imply are the only means we have for constructing an ego and thus our world, we are now in the position to look at Walker's elliptical *Letter from a Black Girl* (1998). This piece can be confusing if one thinks of it as only the artist's fiction rather than recognizing that it consists of several different levels of mediation, since the first section appears to be the distinctly twentieth-century curses (using the legalistic acronym for fornication) of a freed slave who recriminates her former lover/master;

Dear you hypocritical fucking Twerp,

Id just like to thank you for taking hold of the last four years of my life and raising my hopes for the future. Id like to thank you for giving me clothes when I needed them and food when I needed it and for fucking my brains out when my brains needed fucking. I hope that the time we spent in the Quarters with my family sleeping neerby quietly ignoring what you proceeded to do to me- what, rather I proceeded to do to you- ws worthwhile for you, that you got the stimulation you so needed, Because now That Im Free of that poison you call Life, that stringy, sour, white strand you called Sacred and me savior, that peculiar institution we engaged in because there was no other foreseeable alternative, I am LOST.

Before, when there was a before, an upon a time I was a blank space defined in contrast to your POSITIVE, concrete avowal. now, a blank space in the void and I have to thank you for forgetting to stick your neck out for me after I craned my neck so often in your arms.

Dear you duplicitous, idiot, Worm,

NOw that youve forgotten how you like your coffee and why you raised your pious fist to the sky, and the reason for your stunning African Art collection, and the war we fought together, and the promises you made and the laws we rewrote, I am left here alone to recreate My WHOLE HISTORY without benefit of you, my compliment, my enemy, my oppressor, my Love

Should i never be heard from again, follow the Route of my forebears and quietly, GO, or shall I seek to kill you, burning the last of the fuel you gave me and expected of me?

Kara Walker, *Letter from a Black Girl*, 1998, transfer text on wall, dimensions variable

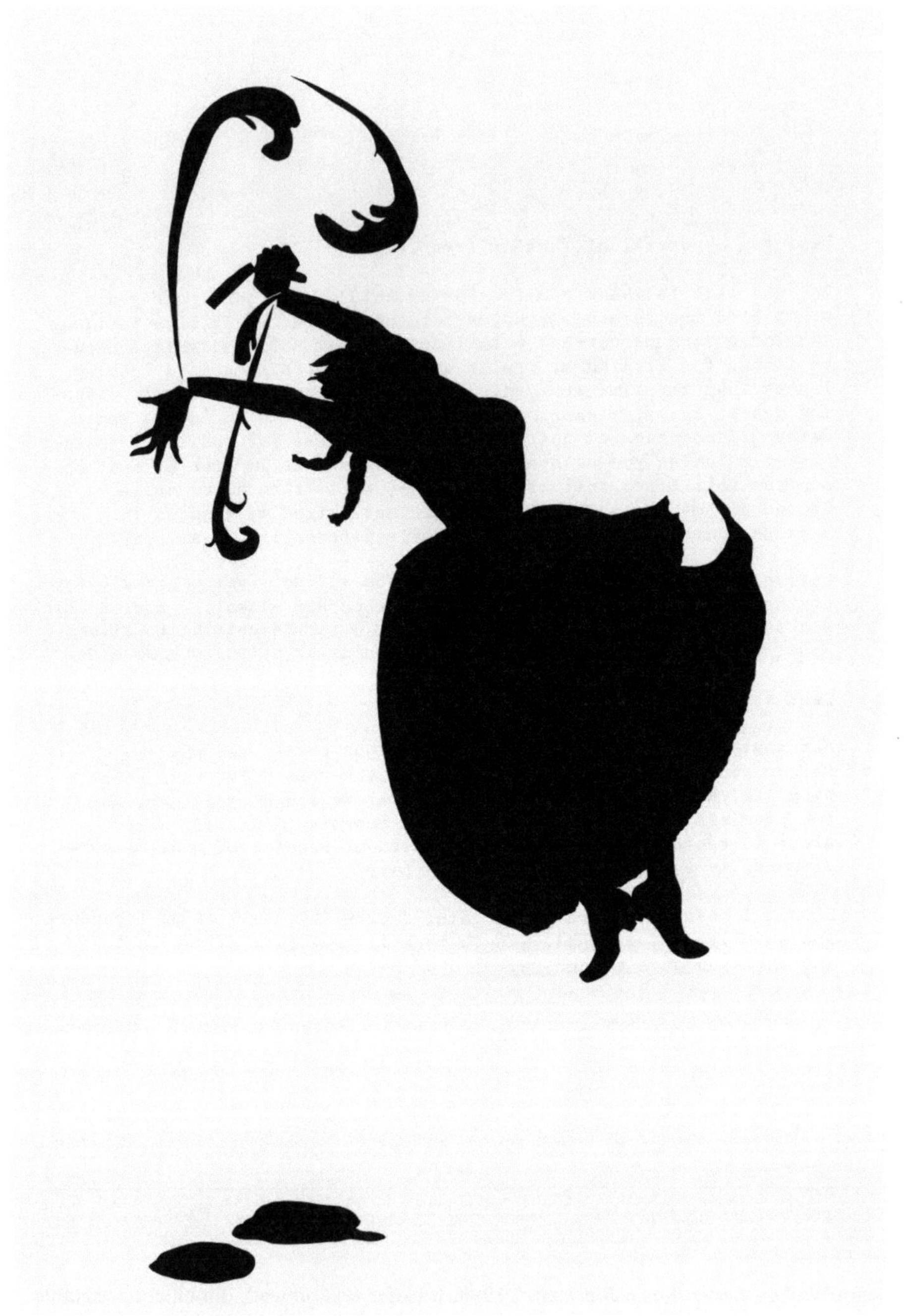

Kara Walker, *Cut*, 1998, cut paper and adhesive on wall, 88 × 54 inches (223.5 × 137.2 cm). Collection of the Walker Art Center

the second portion of the letter is a contemporary Black woman's censure of her upwardly mobile, African art–collecting significant other; and the overall missive is a Harlequin Romance spin on the feelings of both females. In the two sections of this letter, the abject state of the writer is referenced by the admission "I am LOST" in the first part, followed by the resolution in the second that "I am left here alone to recreate My WHOLE HISTORY without benefit of you, my compliment, my enemy, my oppressor, my Love." Again, in both portions of the letter, as in *Slavery! Slavery!*, Walker's alias faces the dismal prospect of having to re-create a new life with the full awareness that one's present subjectivity is as much a sham as the next one will be. The crisis in both the letter and the frieze is an exigency resulting from a false and incomplete view of the world. The only possible way out is a symbolic death, followed by the embrace of yet another shadowy and stereotypical model of subjectivity. The situation is far removed from Ralph Waldo Emerson's hopeful nineteenth-century image of an ever-expanding consciousness, enumerated in his essay "Circles," in which one symbolically dies to the old self in order to be born anew into a more complete, more vital, and greater self.[42]

Walker's art seems to operate in terms of the hopeless condition in which Lacan's and Kristeva's psychology and the weight of stereotypical and ideological views have cast us. This claustrophobic world of never-ending stereotypes may be one of the reasons why Walker chooses to represent herself in *Cut* (1998) as a shadow, dressed in period clothing, who is in the act of slashing both wrists. Abjection, as Kristeva demonstrates, is a form of suicide, an "abjection" of one's present subjectivity. In terms of the recent history of the acquisition and display of blackface collectibles, Walker's *Cut*, with its decorative arabesques of gushing blood, becomes the ultimate piece of Black memorabilia, the one that actually and perfectly mimics its creator's most internal wishes, which are to immolate one's self as in abjection. In the end, the irony of this silhouette's fate is underscored when it assumes the guise of an African American shadow, reflecting the dark side of an ever-ebullient Mary Poppins clicking her heels. The situation partially explains Fanon's observation that "ontology . . . does not permit us to understand the being of the black man. For not only must the black man be black; he must be black in relation to the white man. . . . The black man has no ontological resistance in the eyes of the white man."[43]

But it goes beyond Fanon's binary opposition to implicate the two in an incestuous relationship comprising the dark and light sides of one fictional character. Despite this pessimistic view of the world as a house of mirrors where one image reflects or deflects another and in turn is enslaved by its reflexive state, giving rise to an alienating otherness at the moment the ego is formed, there does appear to exist a slightly oblique space between the image and the abjected self, a gap that could be thought of as a "sidelong glance," using a term that Walker employed on another occasion and for an entirely different reason."[44] This opening between the abjecting self and the object in the mirror stage is a haunting fissure where the Real—that which cannot be symbolized, according to Lacan—has a small but important chance of being discerned. And this enormously difficult job of partially prying open the resisting molds of stereotypical personas to reveal sidelong glances of the Real appears to be one of the major accomplishments of Kara Walker's highly thoughtful, destabilizing art.

Notes

1 Douglas Congdon-Martin, *Images in Black: 150 Years of Black Collectibles,* 2nd ed. (Atglen, PA: Schiffer Publishing, 1999), 3.

2 Holland Cotter, "Selections Fall '94: 'Installations' The Drawing Center," *New York Times*, September 23, 1994, C35.

3 *Ethnic Notions: Black Images in the White Mind. An Exhibition of Afro-American Stereotype and Caricature from the Collection of Janette Faulkner, September 12–November 4, 1982* (Berkeley, CA: Berkeley Art Center, 1982), 7.

4 Ibid.

5 Ibid., 8.

6 Ibid., 11.

7 Erskine Peters, "Stereotyping: Movement Against Consciousness," in *Ethnic Notions*, 28.

8 *Ethnic Notions*, 11–12.

9 Frantz Fanon, *Black Skin, White Masks*, trans. Charles Lam Markmann (New York: Grove Weidenfeld, 1967), 197. In 161n16, Fanon describes Lacan's theory of the mirror stage, which he terms the "mirror period."

10 Kara Walker, untitled lecture, October 24, 2000, School of the Arts, Virginia Commonwealth University. Cf. Betye Saar, "Unfinished Business: The Return of Aunt Jemima," in *Betye Saar: Workers + Warriors, The Return of Aunt Jemima* (New York: Michael Rosenfeld Gallery, 1998), 3. Regarding her own efforts to achieve the rehabilitation of a stereotype, Saar has stated: "The 'mammy' knew and stayed in her place. In 1972, I attempted to change that 'place' by creating the series *The Liberation of Aunt Jemima*. My intent was to transform a negative demanding figure into a positive, empowered woman who stands confrontationally with one hand holding a broom and the other armed with [*sic*] battle. A warrior ready to combat servitude and racism."

11 Jerry Saltz, "Kara Walker: Ill-Will and Desire," *Flash Art* 29, no. 191 (November/December 1996): 82.

12 Fanon writes, "But the collective unconscious without our having to fall back on the genes, is purely and simply the sum of prejudices, myths, and collective attitudes of a given group. . . . I hope I have shown that . . . in fact the collective unconscious is cultural, which means acquired." See Fanon, *Black Skin, White Masks,* 188.

13 Catherine Fox, " 'Genius' at Work: MacArthur Grant Winner Left the South's Shadow but Reflects It in Her Art," *Atlanta Journal-Constitution*, July 6, 1997, O1L.

14 Liz Armstrong, "Kara Walker Interviewed by Liz Armstrong 7/23/96," in Richard Flood, *No Place (Like Home)* (Minneapolis: Walker Art Center, 1997), 102.

15 Ibid.

16 Saltz, "Kara Walker," 84.

17 Fanon, *Black Skin, White Masks*, 112–13.

18 Dan Cameron, "Kara Walker: Rubbing History the Wrong Way," *Journal of Prints, Drawings, and Photography* 2, no. 1 (September–October 1997): 11.

19 Armstrong, "Kara Walker Interviewed," 104.

20 Harriet Jacobs, *Incidents in the Life of a Slave Girl*, The Schomburg Library of Nineteenth-Century Black Women Writers (New York: Oxford University Press, 1988) and Thomas Dixon Jr., *The Clansman: A Historical Romance of the Ku Klux Klan* (New York: Grosset & Dunlap, 1905).

21 Dixon, *Clansman*, 106–7.

22 Saltz, "Kara Walker," 82.

23 Julia Szabo, "Kara Walker's Shock Art," *New York Times Magazine*, March 23, 1997, 49.

24 Barbara Ferry Johnson's *The Heirs of Love,* quoted by Kara Walker in "Kara Walker," *Bomb* 55 (Spring 1996): 46.

25 Saltz, "Kara Walker," 86.

26 Ibid.

27 Szabo, "Kara Walker's Shock Art," 49.

28 See Marcia Tanner, "Kara Walker at the San Francisco Museum of Modern Art," *Art Week* 28, no. 6 (June 1997): 29. Tanner's review includes Walker's extended title.

29 Fox,"'Genius' at Work," O1L.

30 In 1995, Walker had made a panorama that also focused on the Battle of Atlanta. Titled *The Battle of Atlanta: Being the Narrative of a Negress in the Flames of Desire–A Reconstruction*, it was shown at Nexus Contemporary Art Center in Atlanta, Georgia, from May 19 to June 24, 1995.

31 Wayne Craven, *American Art: History and Culture* (New York: Harry N. Abrams, 1994), 331.

32 Walker, untitled lecture.

33 Michael Duncan, conversation with author, September 27, 2001. Duncan, director of the Brent Sikkema Gallery, has worked closely with Kara Walker since the mid-1990s and is an excellent source on her work.

34 Kara Walker, email to author, October 26, 2001.

35 Anne Doran, "Kara Walker: A Dissection from the Bowels to the Bosom," *Grand Street* 58 (Fall 1996): 43.

36 Kara Walker, cited in Alexi Worth, "Black and White and Kara Walker," *Art New England* 17, no. 1 (December 1995–January 1996): 27.

37 Saltz, "Kara Walker," 84.

38 Julia Kristeva, *Powers of Horror: An Essay on Abjection*, trans. Leon S. Roudiez, European Perspectives (New York: Columbia University Press, 1982), 71 and 108.

39 Roland Barthes, *The Pleasure of the Text*, trans. Richard Miller (New York: Hill and Wang, 1975), 68. This extended essay is thoroughly imbued with this concept.

40 Kristeva, *Powers of Horror*, 9

41 Saltz, "Kara Walker," 84.

42 Ralph Waldo Emerson, "Circles," in *Essays* (Boston: Houghton, Mifflin, 1904).

43 Fanon, *Black Skin, White Masks*, 110.

44 Ibid., 82. In response to Saltz's query about this term, Walker replied, "Someone gave a speech not long ago in Washington in which they talked about profiles: the profile of a person, profile as a side-long glance, and I liked that. . . . The side-long glance; it's my answer to the male gaze. It's the little look and it's full of suspicion, potential ill-will or desire. It's a look unreliable women give." While Walker gives the term a feminist reading, it is also useful for characterizing Lacan's Real. In an e-mail of November 12, 2001, Walker recalled, "I lifted the side-long glance from a transcript of a talk Salman Rushdie gave—luckily he's a collector."

Pages 76–85: Kara Walker, *Slavery! Slavery! Presenting a GRAND and LIFELIKE Panoramic Journey into Picturesque Southern Slavery or "Life at 'Ol' Virginny's Hole' (sketches from Plantation Life)" See the Peculiar Institution as never before! All cut from black paper by the able hand of Kara Elizabeth Walker, an Emancipated Negress and leader in her Cause*, 1997, cut paper and adhesive on wall, 144 × 1,020 inches (365.8 × 2,590.8 cm) overall

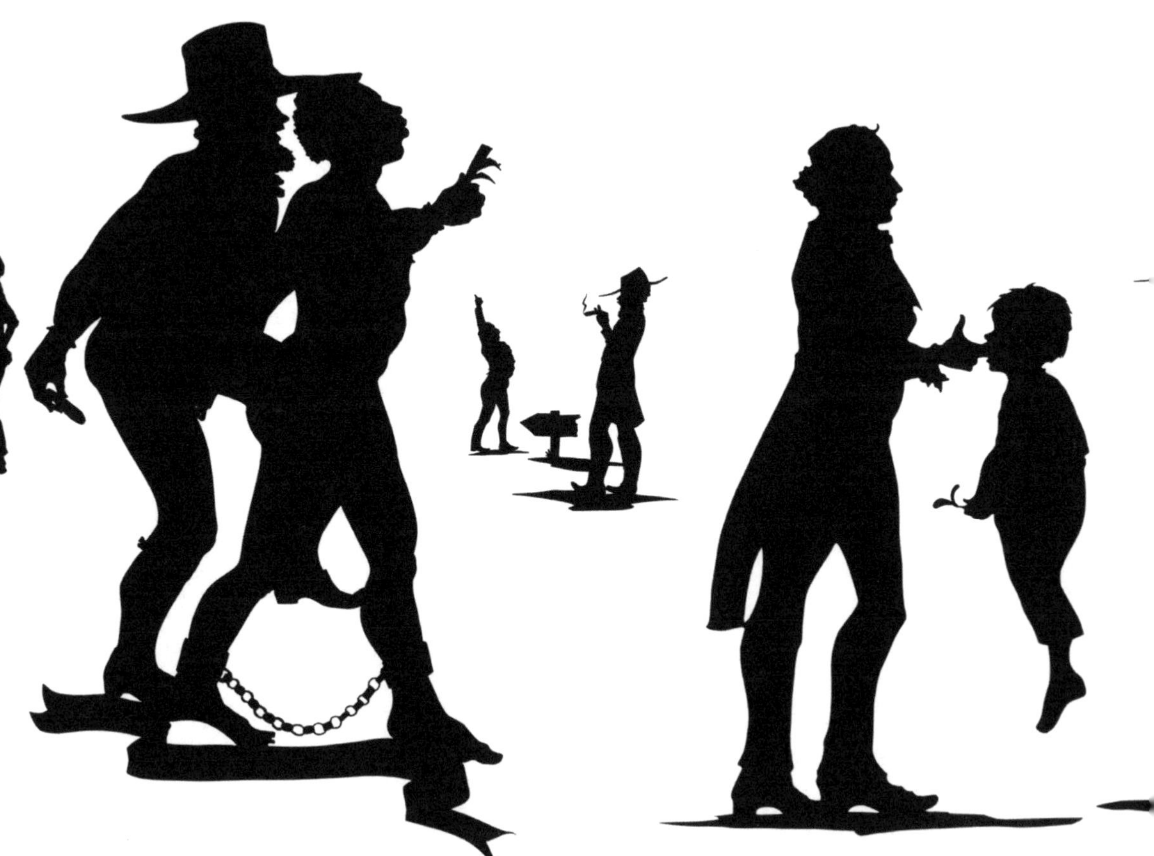

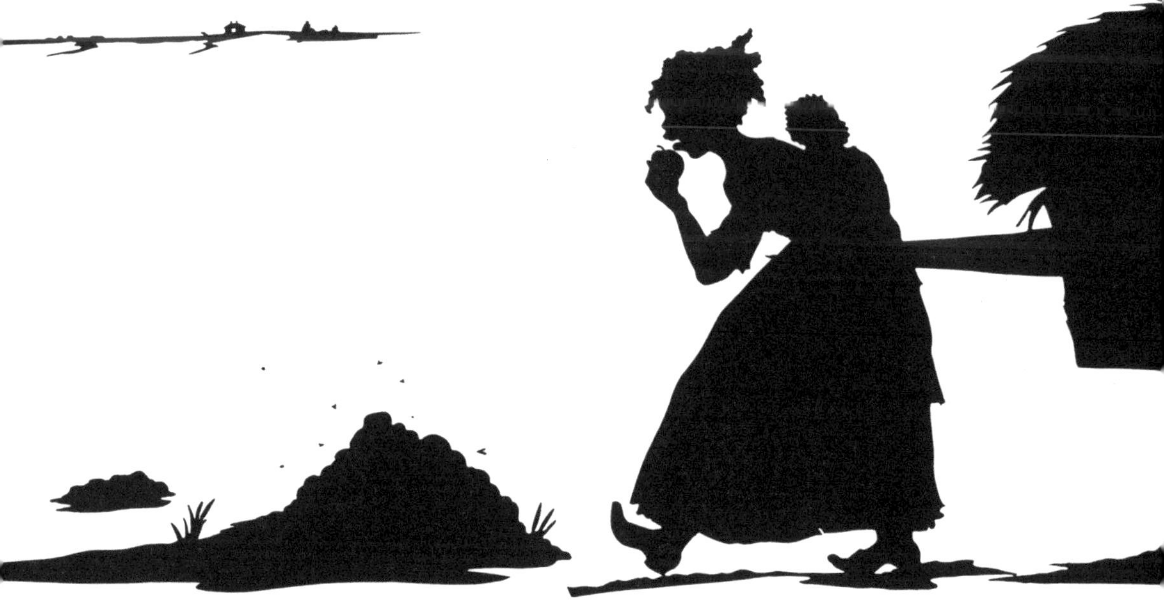

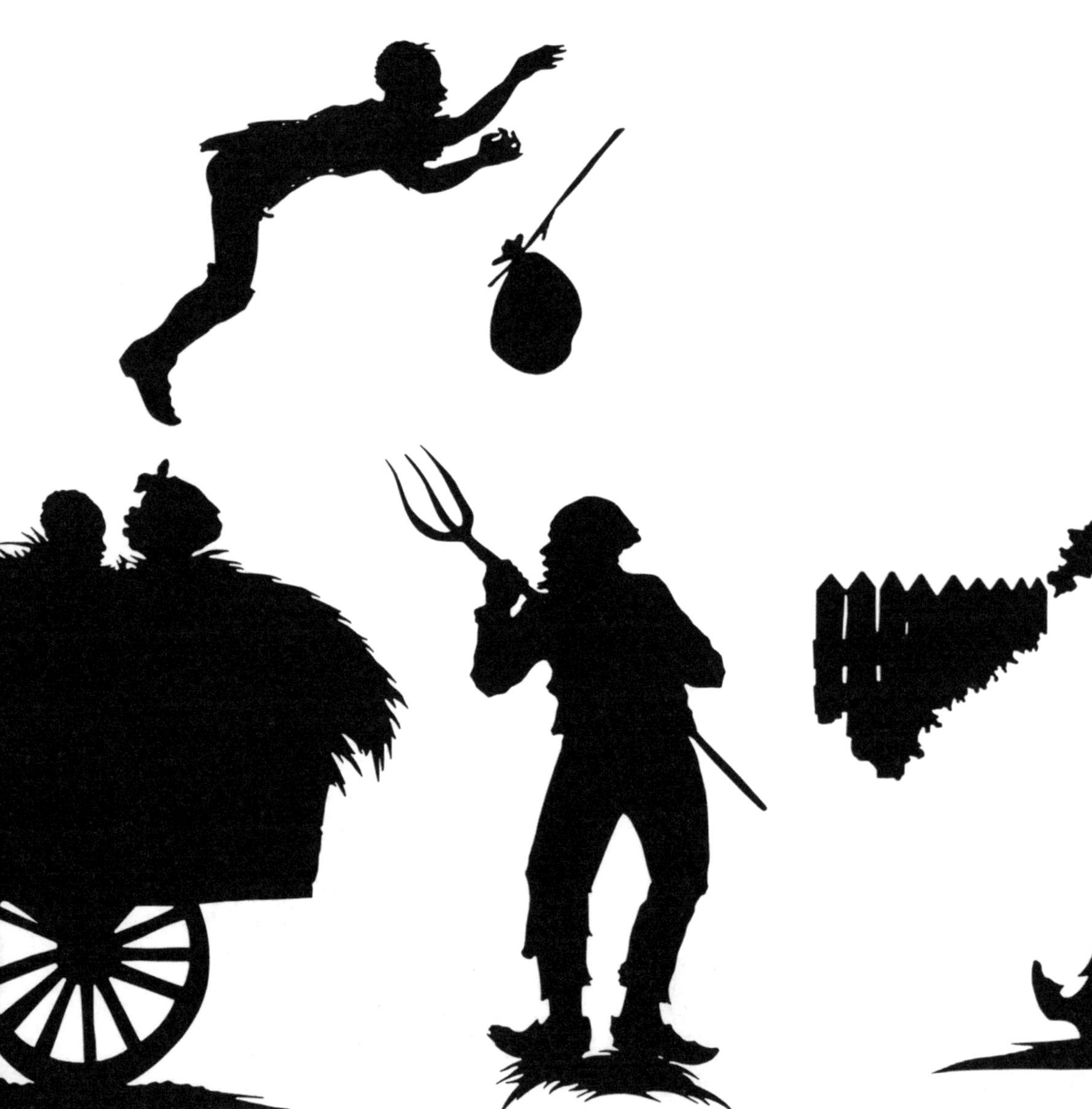

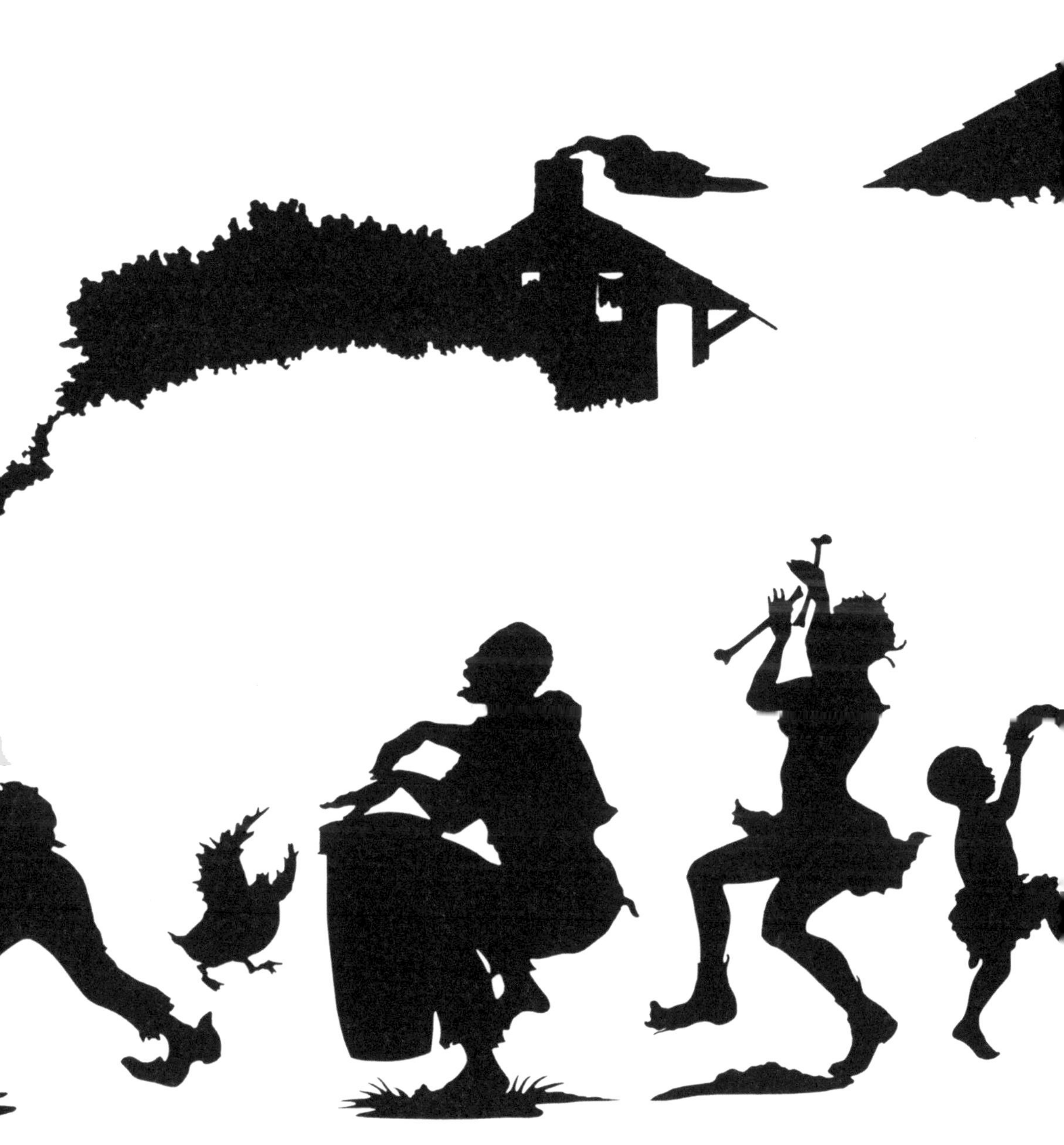

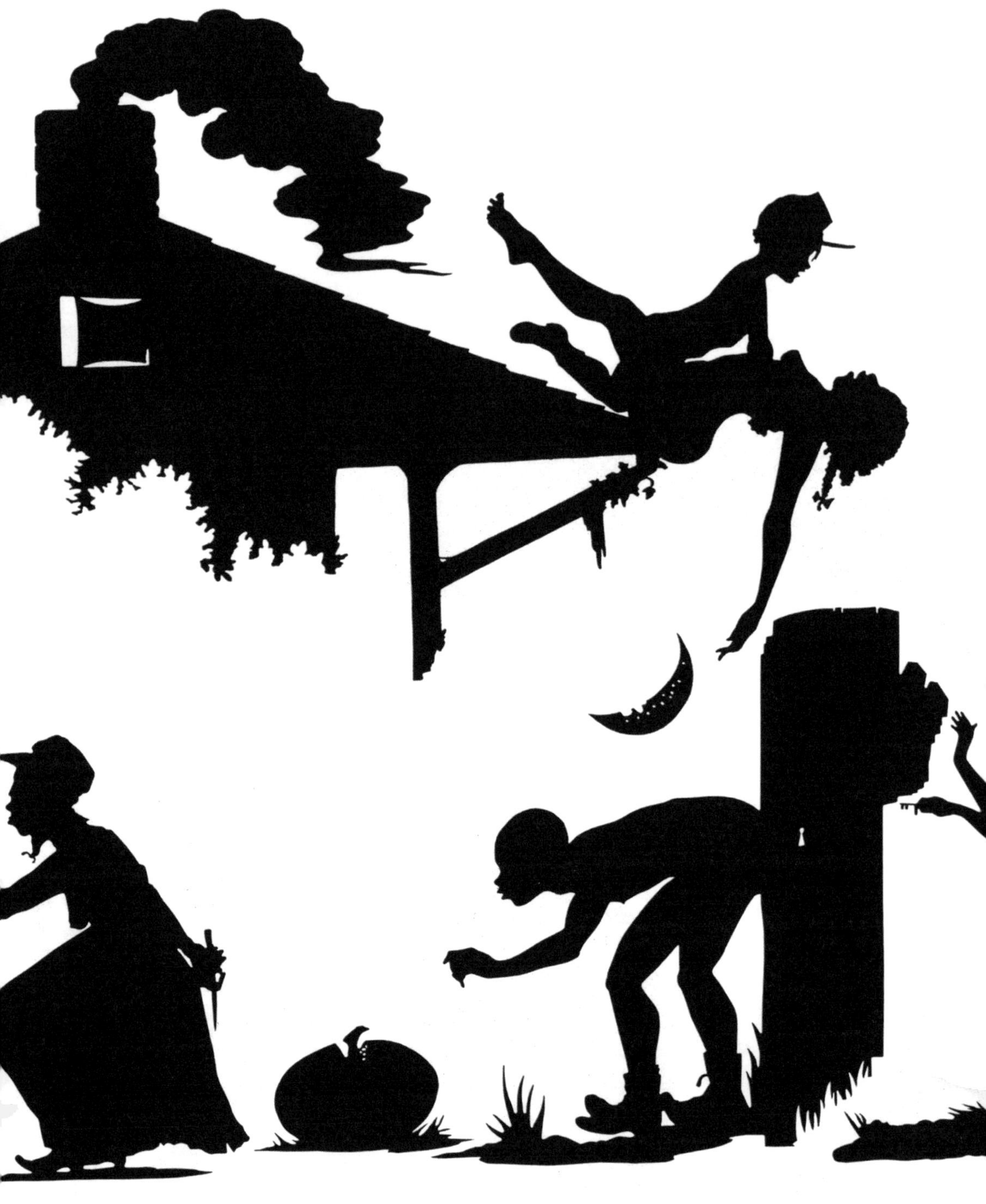

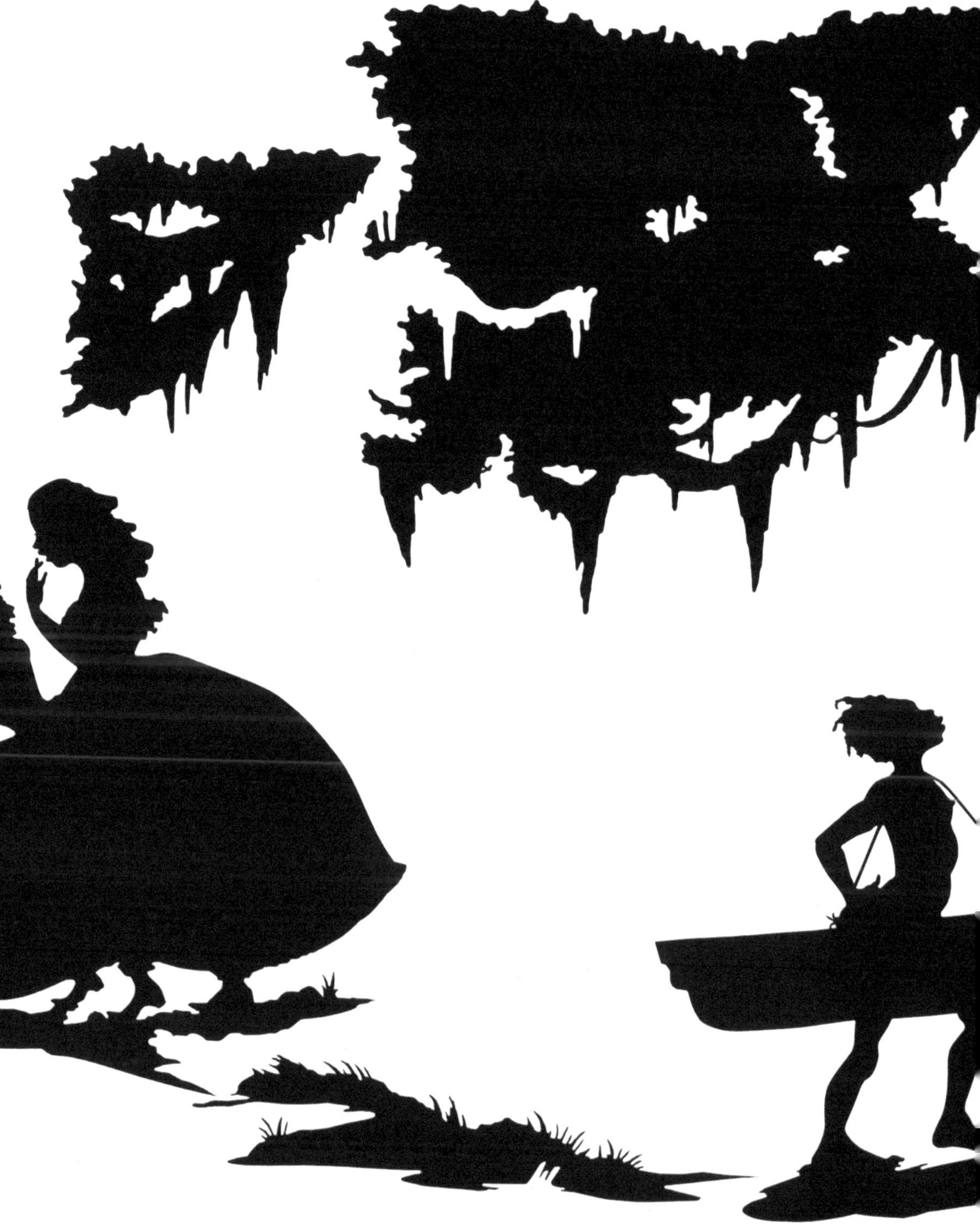

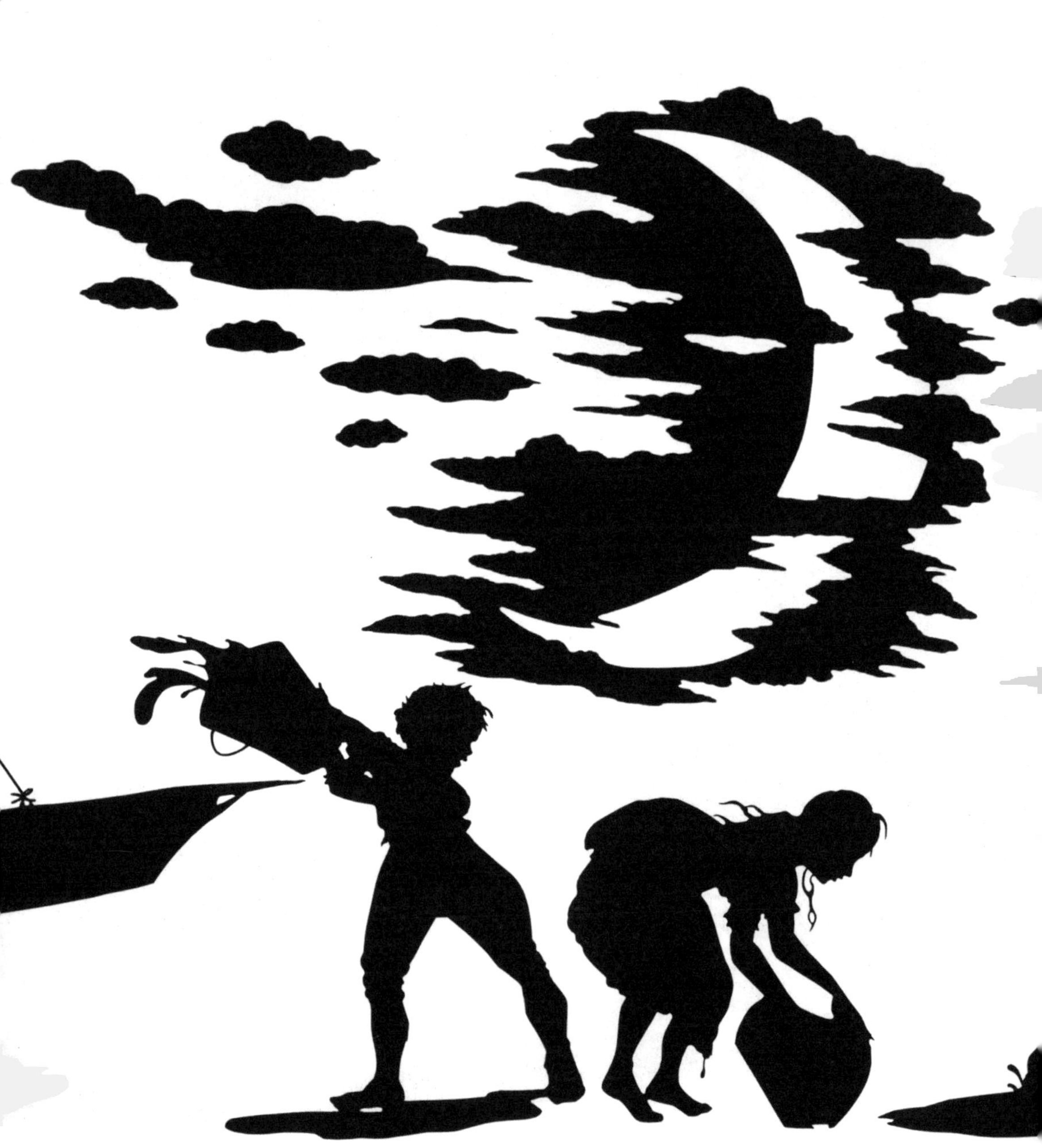

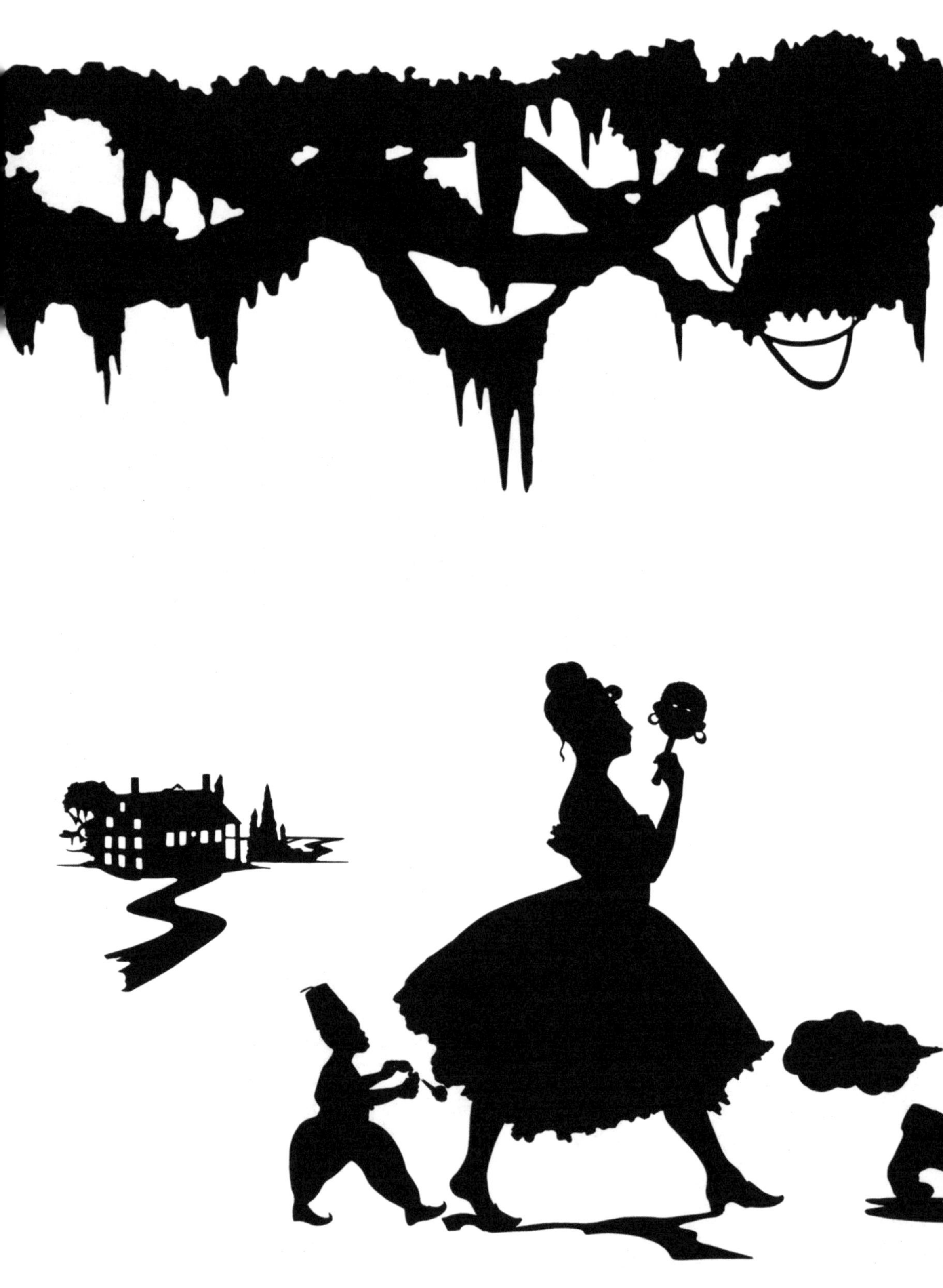

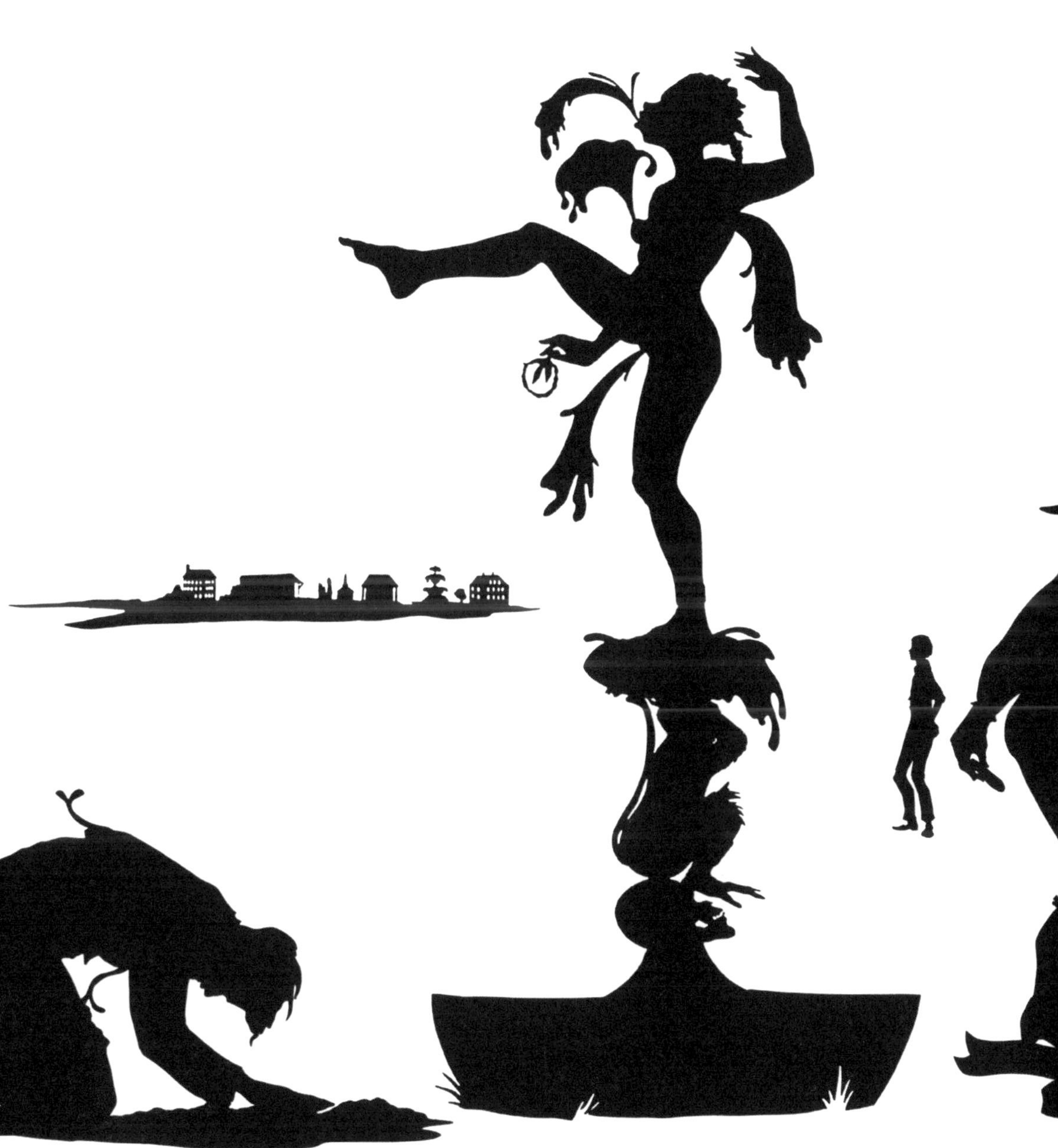

# White Shadows in Blackface

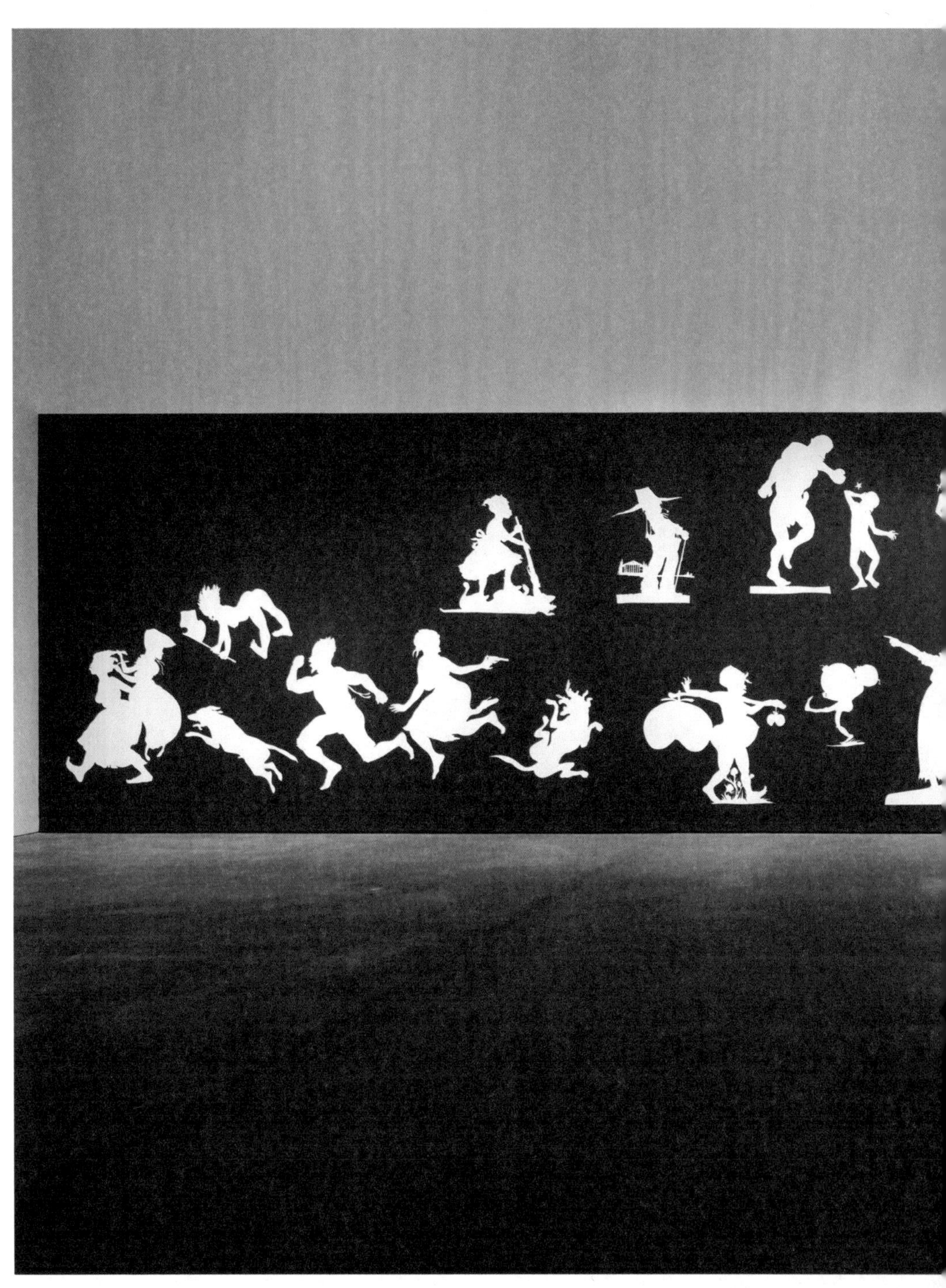

Kara Walker, *The Sovereign Citizens' Sesquicentennial Civil War Celebration*, 2013, cut paper and adhesive on wall, approximately 185⅛ × 787⅜ inches (470 × 2,000 cm).

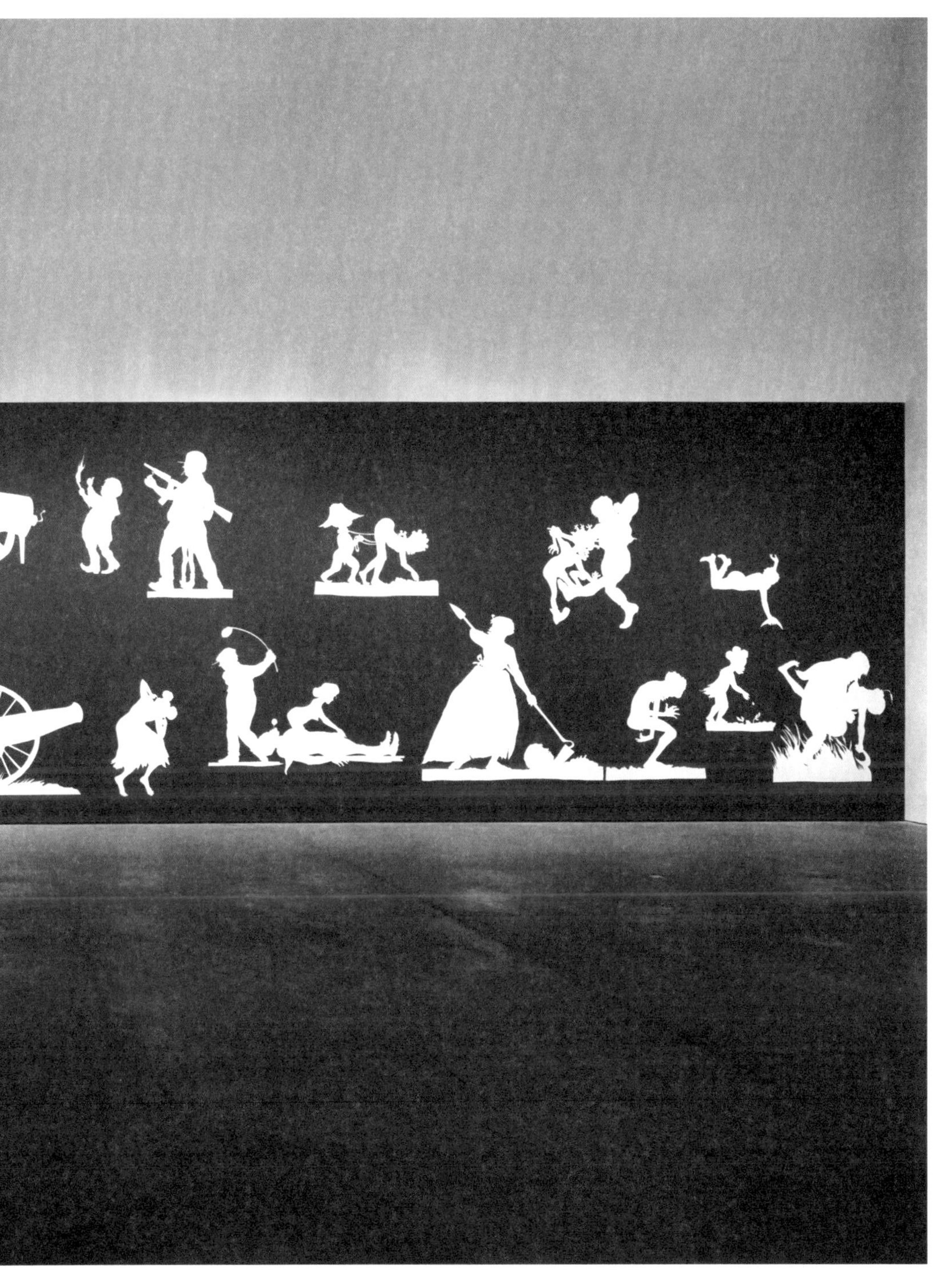

Installation view, Sprüth Magers, Berlin, March 11–April 4, 2020. Photo: Timo Ohler. Courtesy Sprüth Magers and Sikkema Jenkins & Co.

*This essay, which has only rarely been distributed outside Germany, was written for the bilingual catalogue published by the Kunstverein Hannover in 2002 for its exhibition entitled* Kara Walker: For the Benefit of All Races of Mankind, An Exhibition of Artifacts, Remnants, and Effluvia EXCAVATED from the Black Heart of a Negress. *Differing from the previous essay's focus on blackface collectibles and psychology, "White Shadows in Blackface" provides a close analysis of the artist's biographical past and an investigation of a range of historical traditions informing her art.*

—R.H.

*Imagine a country where the entire national population is color. . . . You will have Haiti—the first of the black republics, and that much discussed little land to the South of us. To a Negro coming directly from New York by steamer and landing in Port-au-Prince, the capital, it is like stepping into a new world, a darker world, a world where the white shadows are apparently missing, a world of his own People. . . . It is doubly disappointing then, to discover, if you have not already known, how the white shadows have fallen on this land of color. . . . You will discover that the Banque d'Haiti, with its Negro cashiersand tellers, is really under control of the National City Bank of New York. . . . And if you read the Haitian newspapers, you will soon realize from the heated complaints there that even in the Chamber of Deputies the strings of government are pulled by white politicians in far-off Washington—and that the American Marines are kept in the country through an illegal treaty thrust upon Haiti by force and never yet ratified by the United States senate.*

Langston Hughes, "White Shadows in a Black Land," 1932

*Partly from a love of music, and partly from curiosity to see persons of color exaggerating the peculiarities of their race, we were induced last evening to hear these [Ethiopian]*

*Serenaders. The Company is said to be composed entirely of colored people, and it may be so. We observed, however, that they too had recourse to the burnt cork and lamp black [*sic*], the better to express their characters and to produce uniformity of complexion. Their lips, too, were evidently painted, and otherwise exaggerated. Their singing generally was but an imitation of white performers, and not even a tolerable representation of the character of colored people. . . . It is something gained when the colored man in any form can appear before a white audience; and we think that even this company, with industry, application, and a proper cultivation of their taste, may yet be instrumental in removing the prejudice against our race. But they must cease to exaggerate the exaggerations of our enemies; and represent the colored man rather as he is, than as Ethiopian Minstrels usually represent him to be. They will* then *command the respect of both races; whereas* now *they only shock the taste of the one, and provoke the disgust of the other.*

Frederick Douglass, "Gavitt's Original Ethiopian Serenaders," in *The North Star*, 1849

When Fondation Beyeler's exhibition *Ornament and Abstraction* last year contrasted Kara Walker's *Endless Conundrum, An African Anonymous Adventuress* (2001) with a white-on-white Henri Matisse screenprint from its own collection (*Océanie, La Mer* [1946–47]), it demonstrated how favorably her silhouettes compare with the French artist's late works. Parallels between the two attest to her place in a pantheon of master artists, even though differences between them far outweigh their ostensible formal similarities. In his cutouts, Matisse focused on the aesthetics of presence to create an original, pared-down direction for Synthetic Cubist collages. Walker, by contrast, has invoked the power of absence and removal by creating bacchanals of shadows that bawdily parody mainstream racist stereotypes of Blacks and whites.

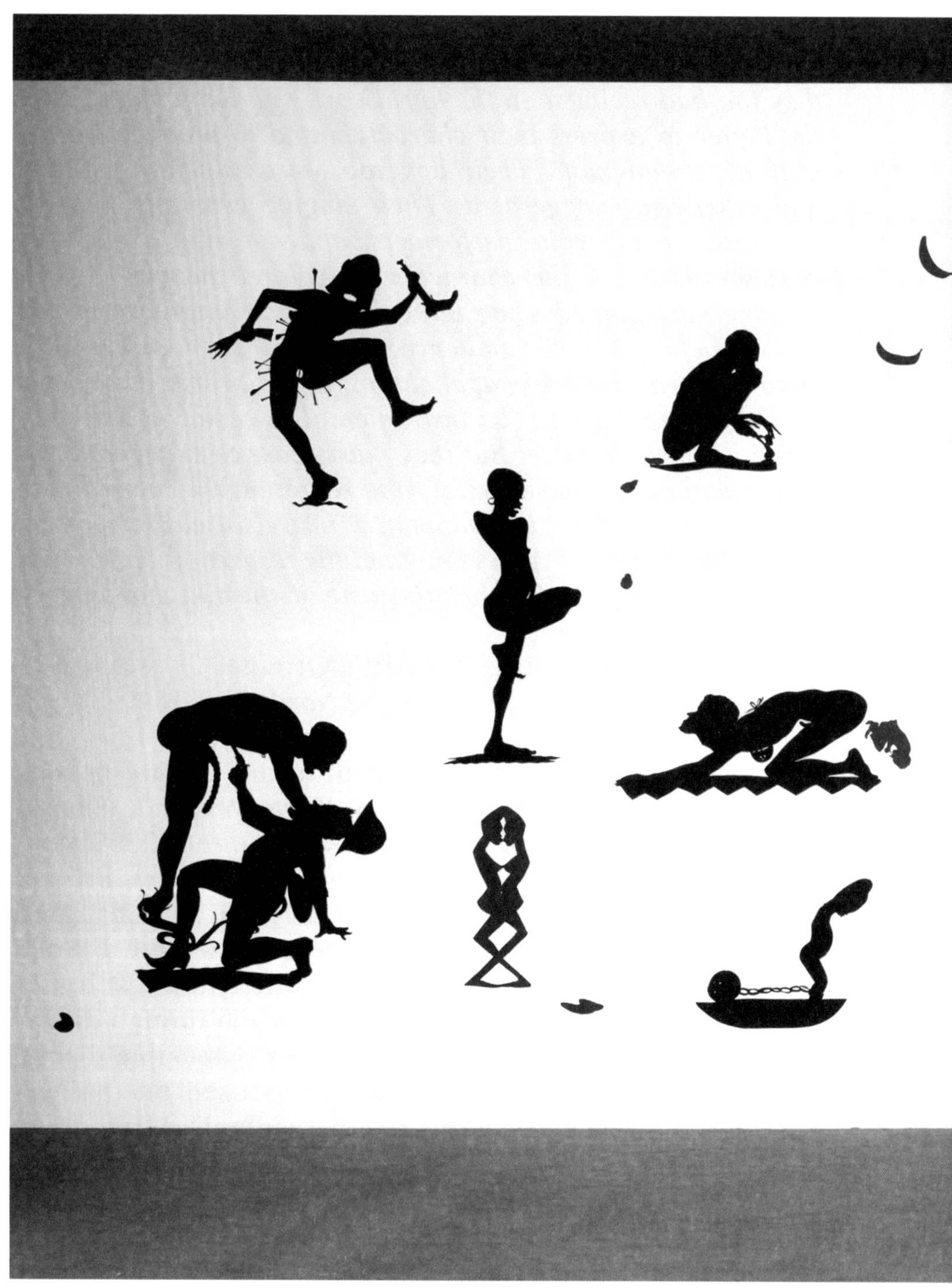

Kara Walker, *Endless Conundrum, An African Anonymous Adventuress*, 2001, cut paper and adhesive on wall, 180 × 420 inches (457.2 × 1,066.8 cm). Collection of the Walker Art Center

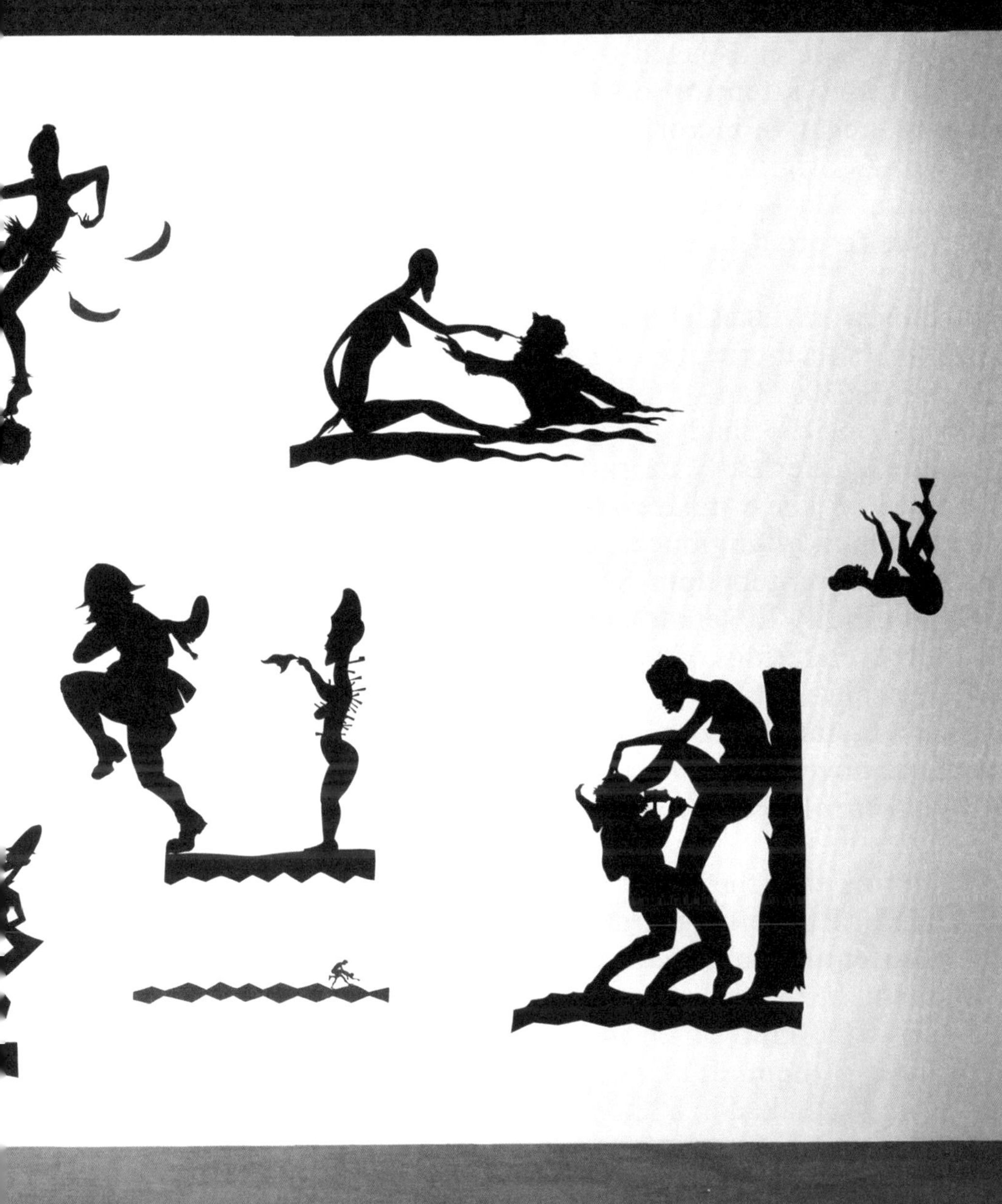

Her figurative art moves from a straightforward representational register to an ideological one. In doing so, it lampoons societal-based travesties and at the same time concentrates attention on the rigid and coercive boundaries of negative pictorial codes that are pornographic in the word's original sense of describing harlots and in the rhetorical sense of conveying the ability of negative stereotypes to prostitute humanity.

Walker's work takes Harlem Renaissance writer Langston Hughes's social critique of partially disguised white dominance in 1930s Haiti—his white shadows—much further by emphasizing the shady ideological effects created by these phantoms.[1] Her early narrative cycles depict stereotypical shadows of slave mistresses, Southern belles, mammies, pickanninies, young bucks, and white masters as denizens of fantastic antebellum Southern plantations, which are in effect dimly lit sets for minstrel shows. Although these shadowy renderings of both Blacks and whites in blackface are farcical variations of known types, they bespeak the artist's often-stated recognition of the ways that mass-market romance novels regularly transform and impoverish reality. As Walker told New York critic Jerry Saltz:

> I think that the historical myths [in my work] are kind of deceiving. I mentioned something about Harlequin Romances. I didn't read that many of them, but I worked in a bookstore long enough to see what kind of an impact they have and who's buying them. It's love. It's desire, all of those things cloaked in a hoop skirt. The only thing that makes it a historical romance is the setting.[2]

In this and other discussions of popular-culture romance literature Walker has singled out the Harlequin series, which is the product of an Ontario-based publishing

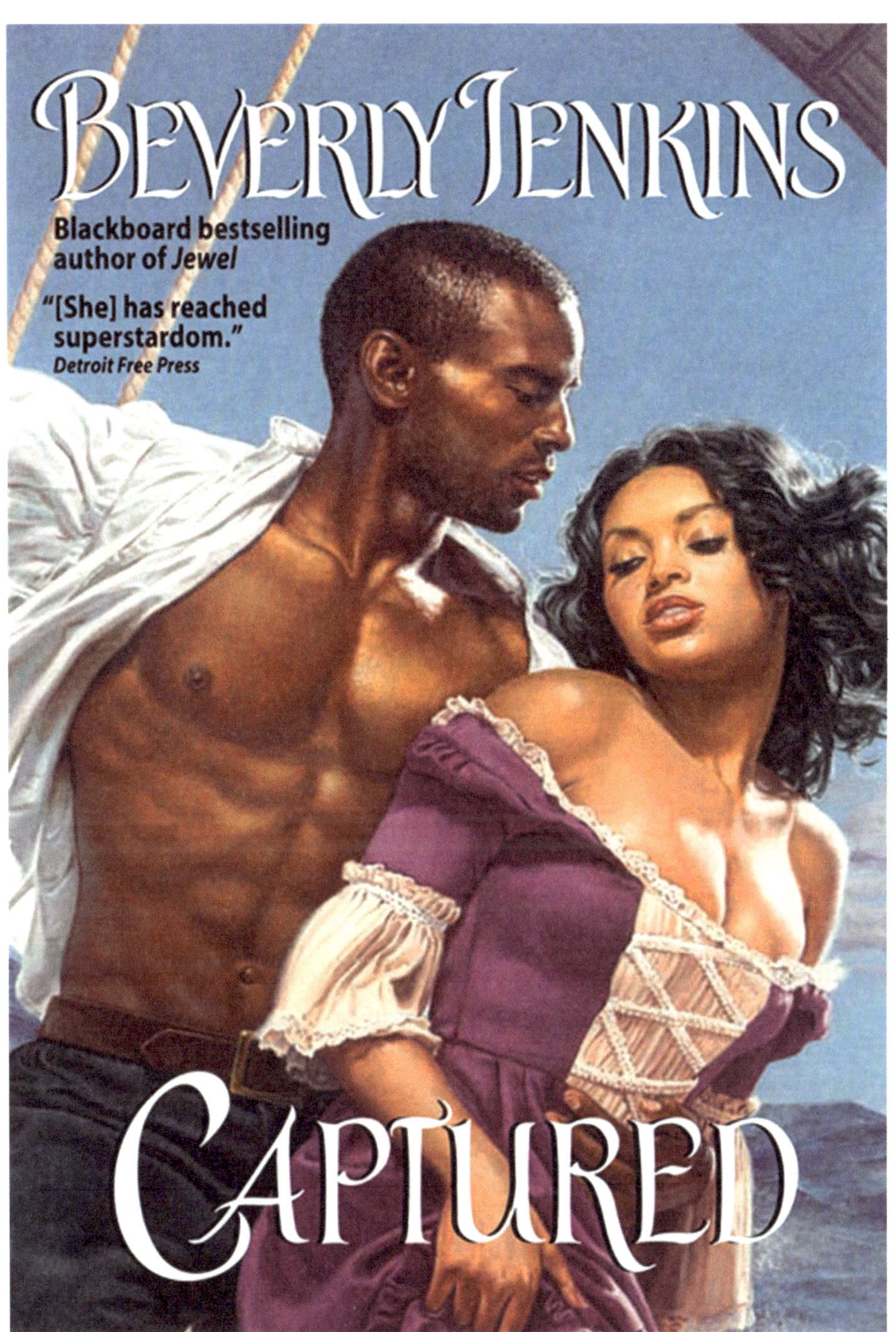


Beverly Jenkins, *Captured*, 2009, Avon

company that began its operations in 1949 as a reprint concern and moved exclusively into the romance literature market in 1957. Forty-five years after the company's inception, Walker first impressed the New York art world with her fifty-foot-long pastiche of Margaret Mitchell's antebellum novel *Gone with the Wind*—a prototype for many Harlequin Romance novels—that she called *Gone: An Historical Romance of a Civil War as It Occurred b'tween the Dusky Thighs of One Young Negress and Her Heart*. That same year of 1994 the company's listings included seven hundred titles in print, and it was able to boast annual sales of two hundred million books in more than one hundred international markets. The publishing house's tremendous financial success can be attributed to its phenomenal ability to repeatedly sell a formulaic approach to fiction.

American and gender studies specialist Janice A. Radway in *Reading the Romance: Women, Patriarchy, and Popular Literature* has summarized this company's innovative marketing strategies. She points out that:

> [Harlequin's] operation is a highly sophisticated version of semi-programmed issue whereby books are produced especially for an already identified, codified, and partially analyzed audience. In fact, Harlequin operates on the assumption that a book can be marketed like a can of beans or a box of soap powder. Its extraordinary profit convincingly demonstrates that books do not necessarily have to be thought of and marketed as unique objects but can be sold regularly and repetitively to a permanent audience on the basis of brand-name identification alone.[3]

The postmodern emphasis on reading is strangely inverted and inadvertently parodied by such category literature as

Harlequin, which set out in the early 1970s to identify its potential public and tailor its books expressly for this readership. As Radway notes:

> Concomitantly, the principal activity of these publishers [subscribing to the Harlequin system] changed significantly from that of locating or even creating an audience for an existing manuscript to that of locating or creating a manuscript for an already-constituted reading public.[4]

Harlequin's acquisition editors approach prospective authors with a standardized story line that has proven successful. It comprises the following components: (1) girl meets boy, (2) the two experience strong positive or negative feelings toward one another, and then (3) they become involved in apparently insurmountable obstacles that together they overcome. Seemingly endless permutations on the same basic plot have been developed for narratives taking place in numerous exotic and glamorous locales. Regardless of setting, all Harlequins adhere to the ironclad rule of always guaranteeing readers happy endings. Every book in its barely differentiated series of Romances, Super Romances, Historical Romances, Medical Romances, and Intrigues—to name a few—must accord with the company's preferred gloss on reality that assumes the formula of charming yet intense romances, gritty dialogues, somewhat plausible scenarios, decisive characters, heroines worthy of respect, and dynamic and sometimes even brutal leading men upon whom these female protagonists can ultimately rely. Because Harlequins are romantic fantasies and not love stories, titillation is encouraged while extramarital sex is strictly forbidden, with the exception of its Presents series. As ideological tools for maintaining the status quo of their mostly middle-income female readers between the ages of mainly twenty-five to forty-five years old, these books are unquestionably reliable: they are steamy yet decorous and passionate yet still circumspect enough to appeal to their readers' conventional tastes.

Satirizing these clearly prescribed and highly codified tenets is the modus operandi for Walker's ribald reworking of the category of eighteenth- and nineteenth-century history painting. The so-called *grand machine* distinguished the top echelon of European academic art because it provided a monumental format for depicting meaningful activities of elevated historical and/or literary figures. As a postmodernist, Walker has looked to popular literature rather than the classics for her subjects. And she has tended to rely on monumental silhouettes as a primary means for characterizing them, so that their contingent status as reflections of reality, i.e., shadows, would be readily apparent. Instead of obeying the rules governing Harlequin Romance novels, Walker dispenses with them in shadow plays replete with scatological excess that deconstruct the series' internal contradictions of prurient longing and proscriptions against extramarital sex. In the course of making these works, Walker transforms a genteel view of the antebellum South into debaucheries of a world gone awry.

Even though Walker has referred to the impact that Harlequins made on her views of mature women's fantasies, there is reason to believe she was familiar with other forms of female romances, including the Simon & Schuster imprint Silhouette Books, a Harlequin knockoff. The audience for this imprint differs substantially from that of Harlequins in terms of the greater number of college graduates composing it, thus its openness to heroines with careers and incorporation of explicit and even casual sexual encounters. Brain child of P. J. Fennell, former Harlequin vice president of marketing and sales in North America, the Silhouette imprint advanced the goal of supplying books in the form of commodities to a known market beyond its prototype by pretesting all romances with a carefully selected control group of two hundred readers. When actor Ricardo Montalbán, the clichéd cinematic Latin lover American audiences favored, would confidentially intone on television in the 1980s the Silhouette sales pitch "the beautiful ending makes you feel so good," adding that these romances "soothe away the tensions of the day,"[5] the effect of his words was carefully geared to the professed fantasy life of a clearly targeted market. Thus, Silhouettes, even more than Harlequins, can be said to incorporate and substantiate the tastes, values, and fantasies of first-world, middle-class, and pre-middle-age women, also between the ages of twenty-five and forty-five, as are Harlequin's projected audience, making it an extraordinarily useful repository of firmly entrenched ideological attitudes.

Even though Walker has referred to this type of literature, her works also play off the seamy excesses of such books as Kyle Onstott's *Mandingo*, with which she is acquainted.[6] The copy for the cover of this best-selling 1957 book, which was almost immediately made into a motion picture, interpolates a readership wishing to view the world in stark contrasts and bold headlines:

> Expect the savage. The sensual. The shocking. The sad. The powerful. The shameful. Human Breeding Farm. Behind the hoop skirts and hospitality, the mint juleps and magnolia blossoms of the Old South was a world few people knew existed—a world of violence, cruelty, greed and lust. MANDINGO brings to vivid life the sounds, the smell, the terrible reality of the slave-breeding farms and plantations where men and women were mated and bred like cattle. You may rave about MANDINGO or you may hate it, but you

won't be able to lay it down, because it is a terrible and wonderful novel! A novel no one dared to publish until now![7]

The present to which this ad copy refers is 1957, a memorable time in civil rights battles for African Americans who had witnessed the year before the successful resolution of the Montgomery bus boycott. *Mandingo*'s excesses may have appealed to racists who were angered by the passage of the Civil Rights Act, which provided the federal government with the ability to enforce voting rights for all Americans and set up a federal Civil Rights Commission with the authority to look into discriminatory practices and recommend ways of correcting them. In addition, this novel furnishes other types of readers with a titillating and sadistic screen on which their anxieties about the effects of integration could be projected, symbolically experienced, and mediated. Although Walker is unconcerned with *Mandingo*'s original readership, she allows its mixture of sex and violence in the antebellum South to suffuse her work with its moonlight-magnolia-and-Spanish-moss ambiance, thereby providing it with an ideological platform for staging her orgiastic scenarios.

There is sufficient justification for terming Walker's use of such pornographic books as *Mandingo* as a means for deconstructing the rigorously enforced proprieties of Harlequins and Silhouettes as a type of "signifying" if one closely follows the way African American studies scholar Henry Louis Gates Jr. qualifies the term. In an essay entitled "The Blackness of Blackness: A Critique of the Sign and the Signifying Monkey," published in 1983, the year before his more extensive work, *The Signifying Monkey*, was released, Gates condenses his theories by defining *signifying* as an African American "trope for repetition and revision, indeed . . . our trope for chiasmus itself, repeating

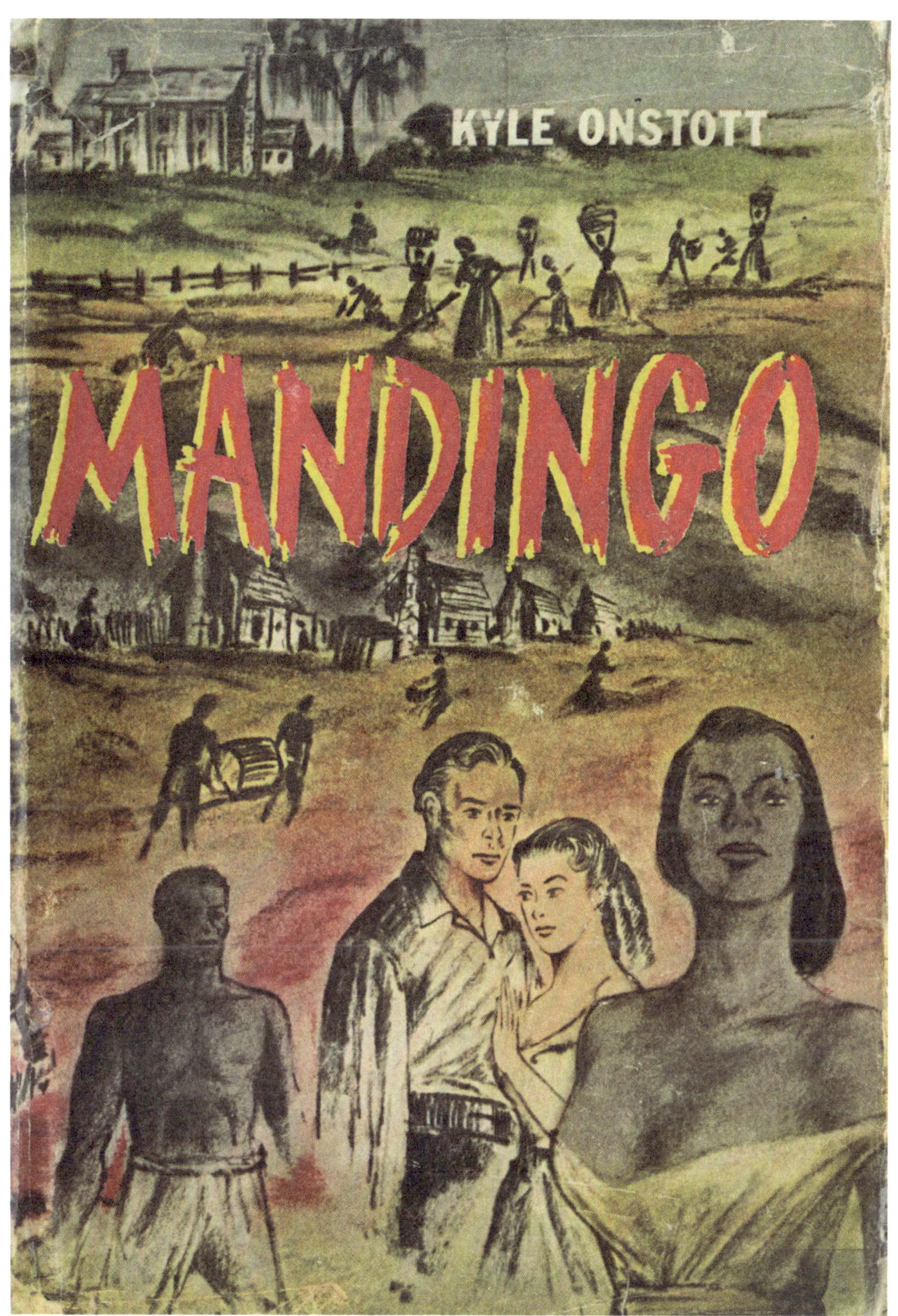


Kyle Onstott, *Mandingo*, 1957, Denlinger

and simultaneously reversing in one deft discursive act."[8] Later in his essay, he abbreviates this definition even more by equating *signifying* with "parodying . . . through repetition and difference."[9] Gates's description of the figurative thrusts of the trickster figure, the signifying monkey, has been heralded as a major contribution to Black literary theory. In retrospect, the success of Gates's codification of this theory can be attributed to its ability to signify for both modernism and postmodernism, since it discerns the essence of postmodernism—an activity that is supposed to root out modernism's essences—to be consistent with African American experience, which he reifies into a playful activity worthy of this infamous folk trickster.

In "The Blackness of Blackness," Gates undertakes the contradictory goals of explicating signifying's operations in terms of such classic rhetorical devices as chiasmus while preserving a distinct ethnic uniqueness for it. In doing so, he inadvertently sets up tensions between classical antecedents and African American usage so that signifying appears to be a distinct historical enactment of the mirror inversions of chiasmus. What makes signifying special is Gates's implication, supported by other prominent twentieth-century Blacks—from anthropologist and author Zora Neale Hurston to American stand-up comedian Richard Pryor—that this process creates a space within the confines of mainstream culture for African Americans to act. Of course, one can argue, as theorist Homi K. Bhabha does, that discernible differences occur whenever subjected groups mime their colonizers since their worldviews are so dissimilar.[10] Seen in this light, signifying is a special occasion of a much more thoroughgoing process occurring in colonial and postcolonial situations. In addition to its affinities with chiasmus, signifying cultivates tensions occurring in postmodern appropriation between established and new meanings that encourage readers to look for intertextual similarities and differences. Walker does this when she hollows out spaces in *Gone with the Wind*, Harlequin and Silhouette romances, history painting, and, as we will see, a number of other established sources in which to parade her cast of shadows.

Her textual insurrection and redirection is chiasmic and appropriative; it is also a form of signifying since mainstream productions are being doubled in order to parody them to unfold a Black perspective. This view characterizes society's ready acceptance of the clumsy machinations of ensconced ideology as incredulous and absurd shadow plays. Even though *Gone with the Wind* is referenced in Walker's first monumental cycle, her work alludes to an entire genre romanticizing slavery that includes Mitchell's saga and Harlequin's many flights of fancy while also going beyond them. These sources include novels by both white and Black fiction writers.

The first story to alert Walker to ways that the enslavement of Blacks can be both legitimized and romanticized is the 1977 television miniseries *Roots*, based on Alex Haley's 1976 book of the same title. This chronological tale, spanning the years 1750 to 1895, purportedly chronicles the Diaspora of the author's own family from Africa to the New World and characterizes it as a journey from slavery to freedom. Although only eight years old when this miniseries made its initial appearance on television, Walker was puzzled by the fascination that both slavery and the antebellum period held for older African Americans. "I don't remember much of the story," Walker recalled to Saltz, "but I know it was very important, we all watched it. Everyone came in to school—it was fourth grade—and started making fun of it. So it became just another joke."[11] Extraordinarily popular, the series attracted 130 million viewers, the largest audience in the United States up to that time. Its tremendous success resulted two years later in the sequel *Roots: The Next Generations*, another miniseries, focusing on the same family and chronicling the years 1882 to 1970. Walker was too young to realize that Haley's narrative of his ancestors' battles against enormous odds enabled her elders at long last to talk about the execrable institution of slavery and their family's participation in it. But she did discern how post-*Roots* African Americans inadvertently began to idealize the legacy of resiliency and strength they believed themselves to have inherited from enslaved forebears. Instead of continuing to be ashamed of their distant connections with slavery, Haley's fans began acknowledging this heritage and searched for ways to research their own genealogical backgrounds by first facing the void that slavery had become and then moving, if possible, beyond the Middle Passage to Africa. Although this acceptance was a distinct gain, it had the unmistakable drawback of glorifying slavery as a sacred myth and essential rite of passage, causing Walker years later to comment cryptically, "black people's 'tolerance' of racial horrors in the past makes them better masochists and more colorful rioters in the future."[12]

For many members of the post–civil rights generation that includes Walker, these discussions of slavery and one's ancestors did not provide the enormous sense of relief they did for older Blacks. Walker explained:

> My experience of the world . . . [is] post-integration. Part of what distinguishes my generation of very young people is that we had to invent another sort of black experience. We were given black pride, Black History Month, multicultural studies in school. I felt that a lot of what I was told to feel about being an African American woman was coming through civil rights documentaries or melodramas

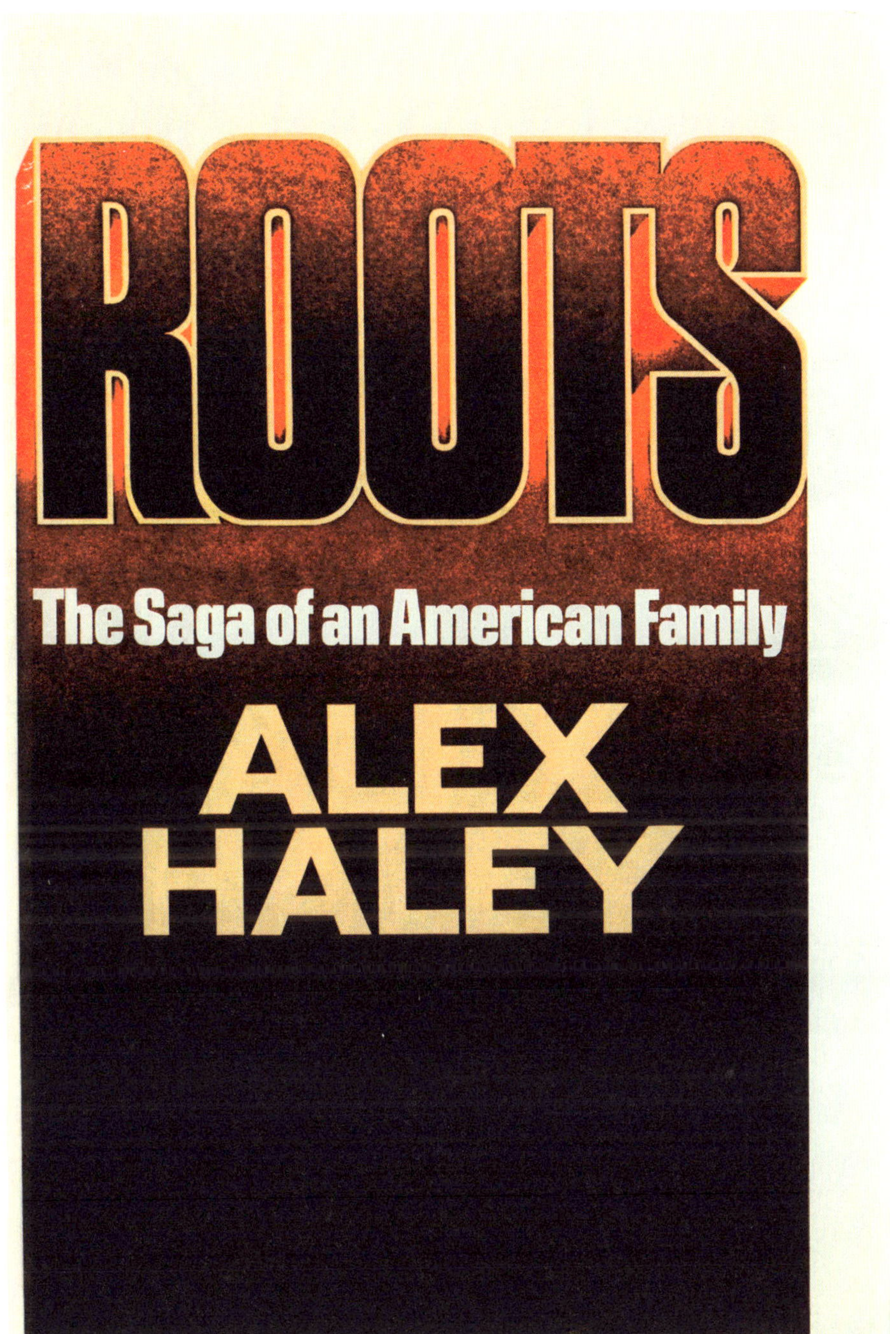


Alex Haley, *Roots: The Saga of an American Family*, 1976, Doubleday

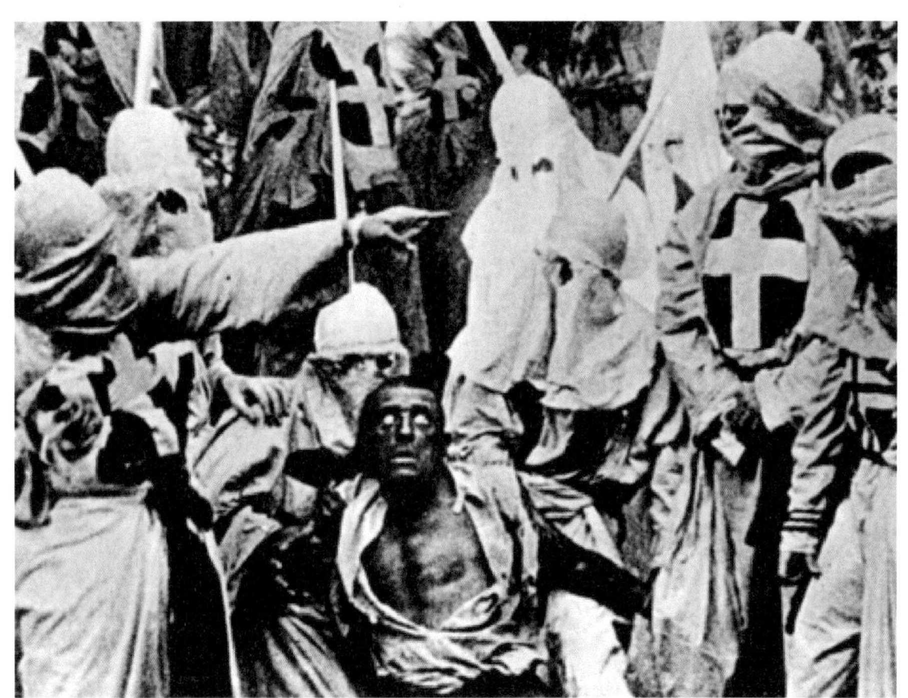

D. W. Griffith, *The Birth of a Nation*, 1915 (still)

> like *Roots*. Yet, not too long ago, black people were being lynched. There is something very palpable about this.[13]

Instead of searching for some distant and essential taproot, Walker and other members of her generation coming of age in the 1990s were more sympathetic to the rhizomatic meandering described by the French theorists Gilles Deleuze and Félix Guattari, in which the self is understood in terms of a never-ending contingency and openness to the social, political, and economic flows assailing and transforming it.[14]

Kara Walker's curiosity about the *Roots* phenomenon might not have risen to the level of cultural critique if her family had stayed in their relatively liberal neighborhood in Stockton, California, located eighty-three miles east of the San Francisco Bay Area and forty miles south of Sacramento. But in 1972 they moved to the South so that her father, Larry Walker, a respected teacher and noted artist working with collaged and printed popular-culture images, could accept a teaching job at Georgia State University. The Walkers then joined other resolute and upscale African Americans who were colonizing the once politically reactionary city of Stone Mountain, Georgia, which was reputed to be one of the most diehard and unquestionably racist places in the United States. Located about sixteen miles from Atlanta, this town is infamous for being the location of the Ku Klux Klan's 1915 announcement of its twentieth-century rebirth. No doubt these revivalists were caught up in the popularity of D. W. Griffith's film *The Birth of a Nation,* released that same year, and its glorification of the Klan's activities. At some point in its history, this group began celebrating its solidarity at Stone Mountain in annual rallies calculated to appeal to a national membership. These gatherings, usually incorporating burning crosses and scores of masked members in attendance, continued throughout the twentieth century.

During the same fateful year of 1915, in which this clandestine affiliation presented itself with a new public face, Helen Plane, a prominent citizen of the town and a charter member of the United Daughters of the Confederacy, contracted the sculptor Gutzon Borglum and asked him to create a 70-foot relief of General Robert E. Lee on the massive granite face of the mountain for which the town was named.[15] Borglum, who later became known for his massive stone portraits of US presidents emerging from the cliffs of Mount Rushmore, convinced both Plane and members of her community that the plan for a sculpture of only Lee was not imposing enough. He conceived in its place a design incorporating the Confederate leaders Jefferson Davis, Stonewall Jackson, and Lee that would be 200 feet high by 1,300 feet long. One of Borglum's major feats was convincing the Westinghouse Company to develop a light projector powerful enough to magnify a slide of his black-and-white design on the mountain's escarpment so that the mock-up would be proportionally accurate. He experimented with greatly intensified bulbs and used tiny strips of black paper cut to form an *X* as a focusing device. The legendary story of projecting Borglum's design to monumental scale may have indicated to Kara Walker that ideologies are only culturally derived images projected onto the world.

The completed carved relief of approximately seven acres known as the Confederate Memorial that Borglum initiated and others completed became the rationale for the 3,200-acre recreational attraction called Stone Mountain Park. At this concession—the most important in the area—is located an antebellum plantation and farmyard consisting of a collection of original buildings built between 1790 and

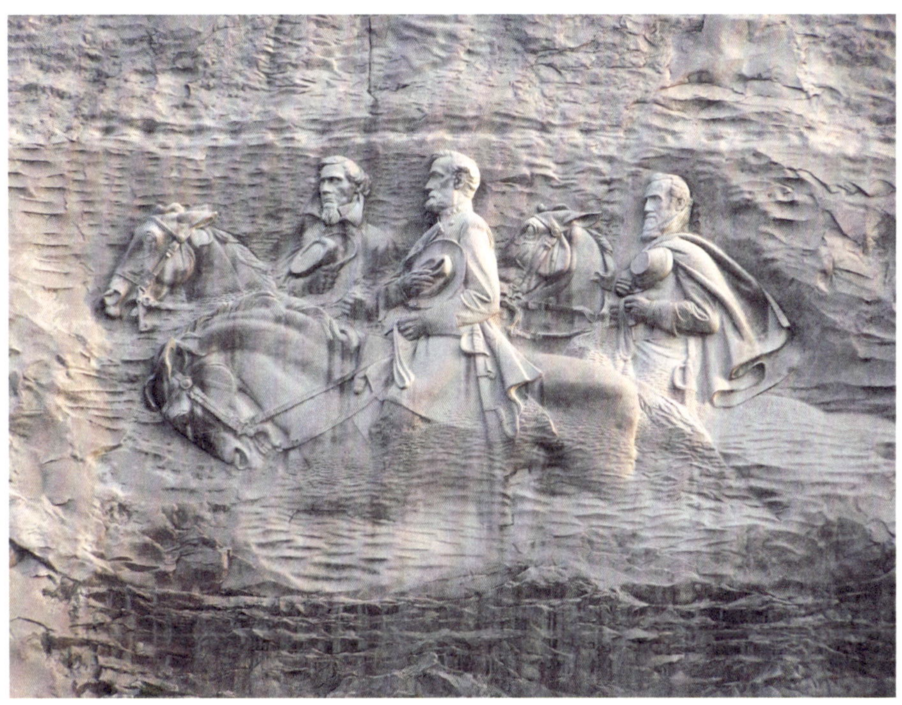

Gutzon Borglum and Henry Augustus Lukeman, Confederate Memorial, Stone Mountain, Georgia, begun 1923, frieze featuring Jefferson Davis, Robert E. Lee, and Stonewall Jackson. Photo: Mark Griffin

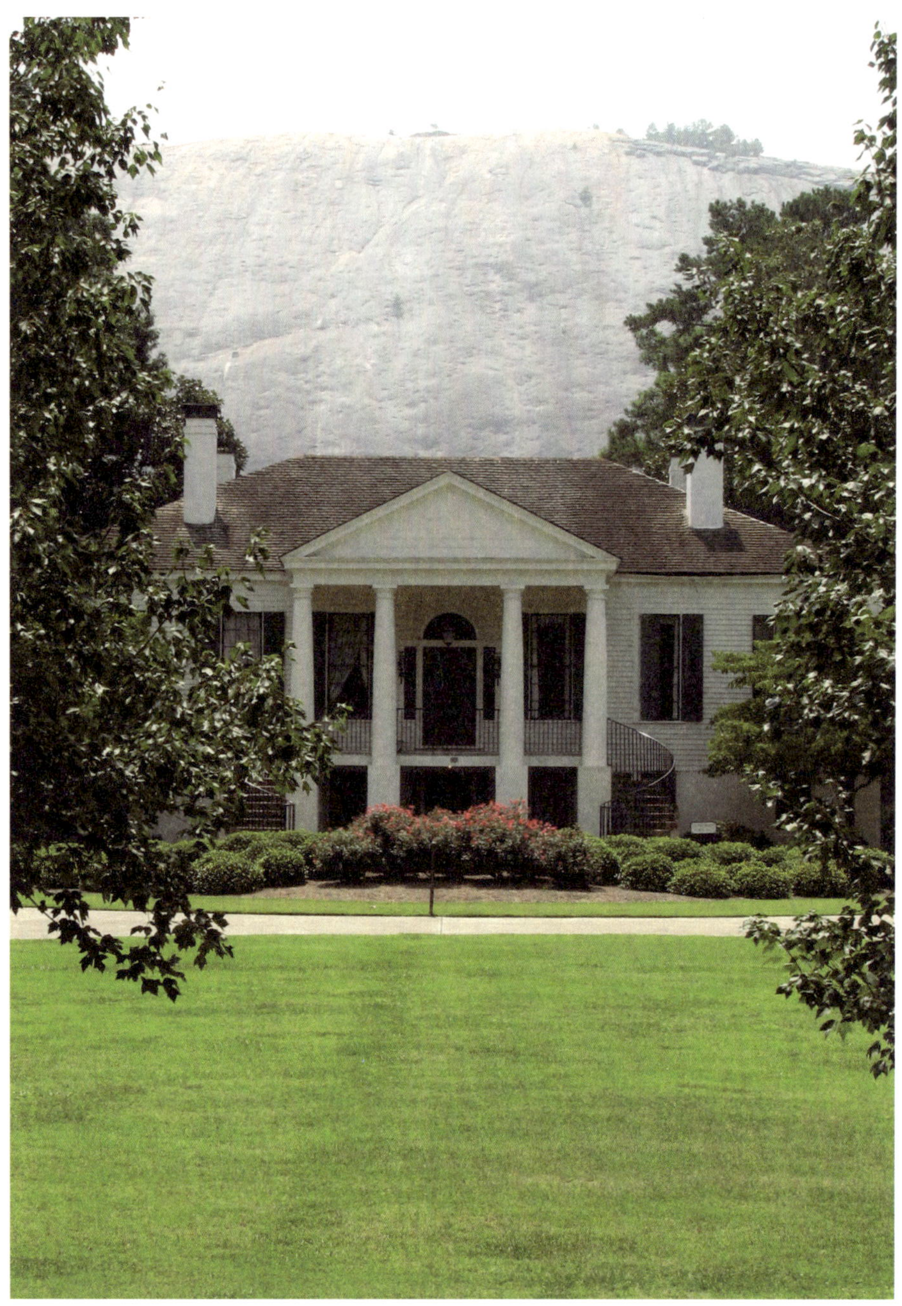

Antebellum Plantation, Stone Mountain Park, Stone Mountain, Georgia.
Photo: Benjamin Miller

1845. In addition to being the home for the Klan's annual pageants, Stone Mountain Park regularly hosts Civil War encampments created by mostly Southerners who dress in authentic Confederate uniforms and attempt to re-create, with as much accuracy as they can muster, the hardships that recruits in the early 1860s would have experienced.

The strange Disney-like atmosphere of this well-advertised attraction, however, is severely tempered for African Americans, who are the prime targets of its unabashed racism. Both Stone Mountain Park and its re-created antebellum setting may have served Kara Walker as a symbol of a clearly circumscribed world where Blacks were supposed to know their "rightful" place, a psychological terrain of dread and outrage she certainly internalized and later branded "my inner plantation."[16] In the following statement, she notes that racism often extended well beyond the confines of the Stone Mountain Park with its Klan activities and Civil War encampments to encompass the entire Atlanta area:

> Miscegenation, race mixtures, causes a lot of anxiety, anger. It depends on where you are, but it seemed very apparent in Atlanta. Hostility seemed very pronounced when I was with white boys. . . . Then there are the silent notes and things from the Klan. It only happened once but it had enough of an impact on me. It threw me from the present happiness all the way into what I thought was the distant past—but really it isn't so far removed. That is where this tableau comes from: as a way to recapitulate all of this and to have some impact on the viewer.[17]

The unconscious and dramatic shift from the past to the present tense in Walker's account dramatizes the shock the artist still experiences in retelling this story, even though the rest of her description indicates her relegation of it to the past.

Stone Mountain Park and its racist enterprises are so blatant in their anti-Black messages that they have effectively kept African Americans at bay. Although such white groups as those congregating around Stone Mountain Park have stated on many occasions their desire to subjugate Blacks, their crude tactics make African Americans exceedingly wary of any attempts to do so and thus thwart these misguided efforts at the outset.

Far more pernicious and difficult for Blacks to contend with are those popular-culture publications and films that delude African Americans and members of other ethnic minorities into unconsciously identifying with white heroes. Frantz Fanon, in *Black Skin, White Masks*, underscores the seductiveness of such popular-culture ideologies that are capable of alienating people from themselves:

> The Tarzan stories, the sagas of twelve-year-old explorers, the adventures of Mickey Mouse, and all those "comic books" serve actually as a release for collective aggression. The magazines are put together by white men for little white men. This is the heart of the problem. In the Antilles . . . these same magazines are devoured by the local children. In the magazines, the Wolf, the Devil, the Evil Spirit, the Bad Man, the Savage are always symbolized by Negroes or Indians; since there is always identification with the victor, the little Negro, quite as easily as the little white boy, becomes an explorer, an adventurer, a missionary "who faces the danger of being eaten by the wicked Negroes."[18]

In the situation Fanon describes, ideology works through mass media publications and encourages Blacks to become blank screens for the projection of white racist stereotypes: at first, they might internalize white supremacist views by identifying with them; only later and very rarely, according to Fanon, do they realize that their complicity results in estrangement from themselves. Their insight, however, cannot take the now-comforting view of W. E. B. Du Bois's "double-consciousness," described in *The Souls of Black Folk*.[19] In this book, Du Bois posits the idea that the Black person can discern himself or herself being seen through the perspective of mainstream culture. But the self is not the natural entity Du Bois assumes it to be; instead it is a cultural construct subject to the whims and wiles of the models it has internalized, which can result, in the most extreme cases, in a type of ongoing paranoia.

Both identification with heroes and collusion with negative ideologies often occur through humor, which cajoles people into laughing about situations that may undermine their own positions. Recognizing the danger of this form of entertainment, Walker has pointed out:

> I have a funny problem with humor, I guess, because I don't consider it fun. I remember cartoons on TV that were old, pre–Mickey Mouse cartoons. These mysterious black-faced mice. I saw new prints of old Bull Durham [smoking tobacco] ads with these coon scenes, genre scenes, sitting on the porch with all the animals. . . . Whatever else they might be, they were also intended to be hilariously funny. The black person was the butt of all kinds of jokes from Vaudeville to Hollywood on up. Where are we now? I think we've stopped being funny.[20]

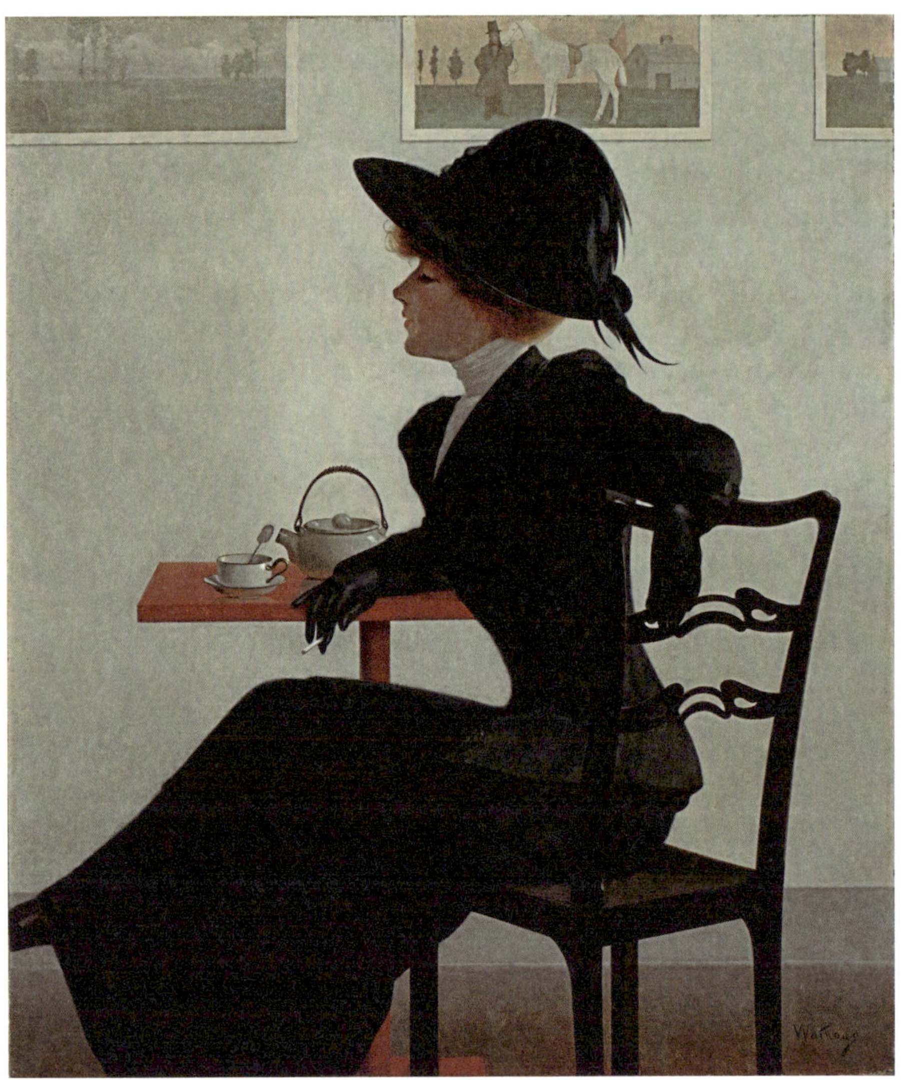

Harry Willson Watrous, *Sophistication*, c. 1908, oil on canvas, 28¼ × 24¼ inches (71.8 × 61.6 cm). The Haggin Museum, Stockton, California

Obviously well versed in many of the pitfalls of internalized racism, Walker stresses its corrupting influence in her art, "My black hole, my silhouette, is informed by these same sorts of 'reasoning' [i.e., not succumbing to the standard clichés for Black people such as being late, eating watermelons, preferring fried food, etc.] as well as the confusion of facing myself as an *undesirable colored person* in the eyes of other people."[21] This emphasis on the silhouette as a void that is found in a number of Walker's accounts—a reading that has nineteenth-century precedents—may have a personal source in her early familiarity with Harry Willson Watrous's painting (c. 1908) of a Gibson Girl, entitled *Sophistication*, that she would have seen as a child since it is one of the acclaimed treasures of the Haggin Museum in Stockton, California. Forming a black silhouette in terms of her huge hat, fitted suit, and schematic Chippendale-style chair, this figure, who is smoking a cigarette, becomes a self-possessed, aristocratic, and white stereotype in contrast to contemporaneous Black stereotypes. The extraordinary contrast between these socially constructed images of whites and Blacks that signaled well-established social polarities in turn-of-the-twentieth-century America no doubt affected Walker deeply with the ways that the color black can conjure images of supreme glamour and nonchalance in the Gibson Girl while conveying the idea of a perpetual underclass when used for African Americans. This contrast, which was one of the polarities of popular imagery of this time, is without question an important source for Walker's work.

Somewhat related to the silhouette's oxymoronic state of appearing both full and empty and the color black's ability to convey images of elegance as well as rudeness is the Silhouette and Harlequin Romance novels' penchant for titillating readers with stories of women gladly succumbing to the masterful dominance of prepossessing males, causing them ultimately to fantasize about their own enslavement. As Walker commented, "My work is intended to function like Harlequin Romance novels, which veil themselves in history and encourage women to participate in stories that are not in their best interests."[22] In this statement, she does not explain how she removes this veil of reality in her art through a program of deliberate abstraction and satirization since her work makes this abundantly clear.

Because racism's greatest weapons for enslaving a group are vicarious forms of identification resulting in self-alienation and self-censorship—not blunt force, as is commonly assumed—it follows that stories capable of beguiling and seducing readers into accepting their fictions as reality are among the most corrupting and effective ideological tools. Since *Gone with the Wind* has proven to be a particularly effective means for inculcating readers in a host of exploitative and depreciative images that have been perpetuated in a great many romance novels, Kara Walker made the deconstruction of its pejorative unity her first priority when she began creating narrative cycles.

The obligation to do so was dramatized at the time by the repeated attempts of civic leaders in the Atlanta area to create a $50 million *Gone with the Wind* theme park. They were hoping to build a postmodern spectacle similar to the types that semiotician Umberto Eco labeled "hyperreality"[23] by reconstructing only the parts of the plantation houses Tara and Twelve Oaks that are shown in the film, as well as Rhett Butler's mansion and other sites memoralized in Margaret Mitchell's book. In metropolitan Atlanta, Clayton, Douglas, and Henry counties were each contending for the right to put together a *GWTW* recreational area in time to take advantage of the anticipated crowds who would be attending the 1996 Summer Olympics. There was even talk of incorporating the three-sided stage set of Tara used in the film, which Georgia's former first lady Betty S. Talmadge had purchased in 1979. The prospective organizers of this park reasoned that since this house had become equated in many people's minds with their image of the South, it would be seen as more real than an actual plantation house from the antebellum era. But to questions regarding the possibility of sugarcoating slavery, the organizers responded that they were focusing on the movie, not history. These discussions concerned with the ramifications of the shadowy world of film corroborate the theories of French sociologist Jean Baudrillard, who describes simulation as the replacement of reality by competing models for it.[24] At the same time as the *GWTW* theme park was being anticipated, the nonprofit organization known as the Margaret Mitchell House Inc. was seeking a $1–3 million sum to restore and thus immortalize the residence that Mitchell herself had called "The Dump."

The irony of basing history on cinematic versions of it has been readily appreciated by Walker, who has created flagrantly orgiastic visions of the South that, among other things, characterize the unnatural coupling of history and romance into an acknowledged type of fiction in terms of a grand debauchery. No doubt she has needed to exaggerate her subject in order to critique it. Similar to other ironic critiques that laminate distinct realities onto one another so that readers can discern the layers composing these new and unnatural affiliations, Walker joins elements of truth with cartooned versions of it to articulate the essentially pornographic nature of this new historic simulacrum.

Although Harlequins represent a deodorized version of the Old South that accords with the tepid preferences of its readership, the antebellum South, particularly in Virginia and Kentucky, was far from the mythic Eden depicted in Civil

War novels. In its often harsh business tactics, the antebellum South was removed from the heightened eroticism and blatant sadism of the slave-breeding plantation represented in *Mandingo*. In fact, in the 1850s, it was an efficiently organized and little discussed seedbed for the regular impregnation of female slaves by both Blacks and whites in order to meet the increasing demands for more slaves to grow and pick cotton in the booming frontier slave states of Alabama, Mississippi, and Louisiana. In the decade before the Civil War, when the importation of West African slaves had been outlawed for over four decades, the number of mulatto slaves is estimated to have increased 66.9 percent.[25]

As the astute chronicler Mary Boykin Chesnut of Charleston noted at the time:

> God forgive us, but ours is a monstrous system, a wrong and an iniquity. Like the patriarchs of old, our men live all in one house with their wives and their concubines; and the mulatto children one sees in every family partly resemble the white children. Any lady is ready to tell you who is the father of all the mulatto children in everybody's household but her own. Those, she seems to think, drop from the clouds.[26]

While responding to the escalating need for slaves in developing antebellum cotton plantations in Mississippi and Alabama helped defray expenses for well-established plantations in Virginia, where the land had been depleted by too much tobacco farming, the significant increase in the number of mulatto slaves in the decades leading up to the Civil War created enormous problems in the South. Specifically, it blurred the clearly marked lines separating whites as self-proclaimed masters and their slaves, whom they had relegated to subhuman status. The subsequent enactment

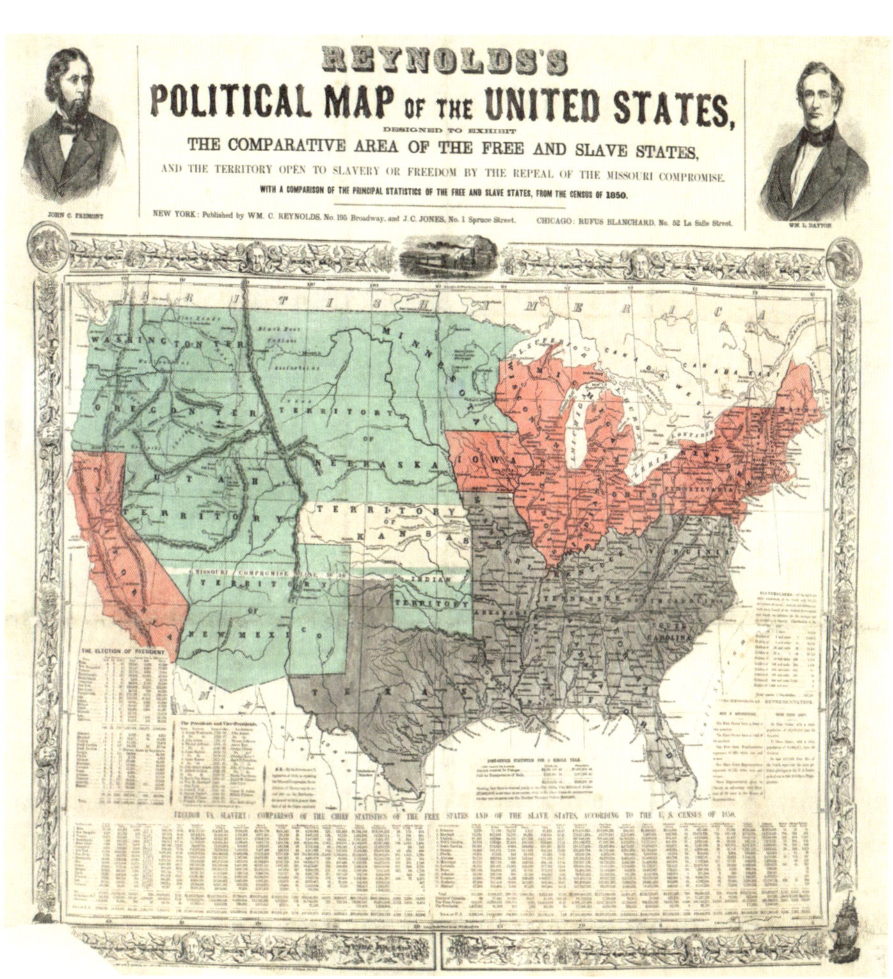


Reynolds's Political Map of the United States, 1856

of the "one-drop rule," which declared all mulattos to be legally categorized as "Negroes," exacerbated rather than alleviated race relations, since it ignored an intense and ambiguous middle ground that was coming to the fore. In consideration of this ruling, it is of interest to note that Walker makes all figures inhabiting her work, regardless of their ethnic affiliations, into black silhouettes. The implication is that the institution of slavery is itself a shadowy realm that joins together all those who participate in it.

Walker's work is far removed from the essentializing, modernist view of 1960s-era African Americans who proclaimed "black is beautiful." Her approach to Blackness is closer to the parody of the "blackness of blackness" prologue in Ralph Ellison's *Invisible Man*, summarized by Gates in the following manner:

> As Ellison's text states, "black is" and "black ain't." "It do, Lawd," "an' it don't." Ellison parodies here the notion of essence, of the supposedly natural relation between the symbol and the symbolized. The vast and terrible Text of Blackness, we realize, has no essence; rather it is signified into being by a signifier.[27]

Similar to Ellison's parody, Walker's work presents *black* as a destabilized term whose meaning ricochets back and forth among a number of variables. This assessment correlates with her conclusion that

> the silhouette speaks a kind of truth. It traces an exact profile, so in a way I'd like to set up a situation where the viewer calls up a stereotypic response to the work—that I, black artist/leader, will "tell it like it is." But the "like it is," the truth of the piece, is as clear as a Rorschach test.[28]

Part of Walker's overall program has included the need to defuse the highly cathected view of Blacks that unnecessarily perpetuates the state of otherness. As she told critic Alexi Worth:

> So it was an ironic and giddy, half-vulgar attempt on my part to suggest that everything is akin to blackness. Thus the silhouette. A benign middle-class art form with higher aspirations, a minstrel show, a psychological revelation, the shadow knows, you know.[29]

Although concluded in a joking manner with a reference to a popular radio program called *The Shadow* that ran from 1937 to 1954, Walker's free association of types should not be used to undermine the seriousness of purpose that guides her desire to make Blackness such an ultimate signifier that it disqualifies itself. As the above statement implies, her works are intended to bring about a necessary leveling so that racial slurs, including perhaps the highly combative "N-word," can no longer incite Blacks with the force they have in the past.[30] In this way, racism is directed away from its intended victims and aimed instead at the white shadows invoking it.

Even though corroboration for viewing whites as silhouettes is certainly not needed, since an ideological reading provides ample justification, it is of interest to note the thematization of silhouettes found in the film *Gone with the Wind* since Walker's first narrative cycle *Gone* . . . , as mentioned earlier, parodied it. Near the beginning of the film, the scene with Scarlett and her father, Gerald, framed by a giant oak and gazing at Tara in the middle distance, simulates contemporary, mass-produced, convex-glass silhouettes that contrast two-dimensional reverse-painted-on-glass images with painted three-dimensional-looking backdrops or photographed scenes. Later, when Scarlett delivers her sister-in-law Melanie's baby during the Yankee attack on Atlanta, the two assume the semblance of dramatic shadows. Soon thereafter in the film, both the famous escape during the burning of Atlanta and the goodbye kiss between Scarlett and Rhett are memorialized as silhouettes, as is the melodramatic tableau of Scarlett foraging for turnips in the depleted garden of Tara and declaring her resolve never to be hungry again. In these last scenes, a strong red light, functioning no doubt as a metonymic trope for Scarlett's name and burgeoning personality, enhances the drama so that this now larger-than-life female protagonist can become an adequate emblem for war-torn Georgia and the Reconstruction era. In each of these situations, silhouettes are used as a means for briefly suspending action and crystallizing particularly climactic events formative to Scarlett's developing character. In this manner, they are hopefully fixed in the moviegoer's memory with a clarity similar to the ways in which traditional silhouettes arrest contours of particular individuals' visages, making them easy to remember. In much this same manner, Walker has recently taken to employing colored gels in such pieces as *Insurrection! (Our Tools Were Rudimentary, Yet We Pressed On)* (2000), *Darkytown Rebellion* (2001), and *Miss Merrimac and the Monitor* (2001), where the use of ambient color heightens the dramatic effects of the work and intensifies the theatricality of its stereotypical subject matter.

Thus far, this discussion of Kara Walker's work has tended to rely on the artist as the central and self-conscious director of her work. However worthwhile this approach is, I should point out that the assumption of artistic self-consciousness and accountability has both its advantages and disadvantages. It provides the obvious benefit of encouraging us to become well acquainted with the artist and her point of view as well as her motivations and

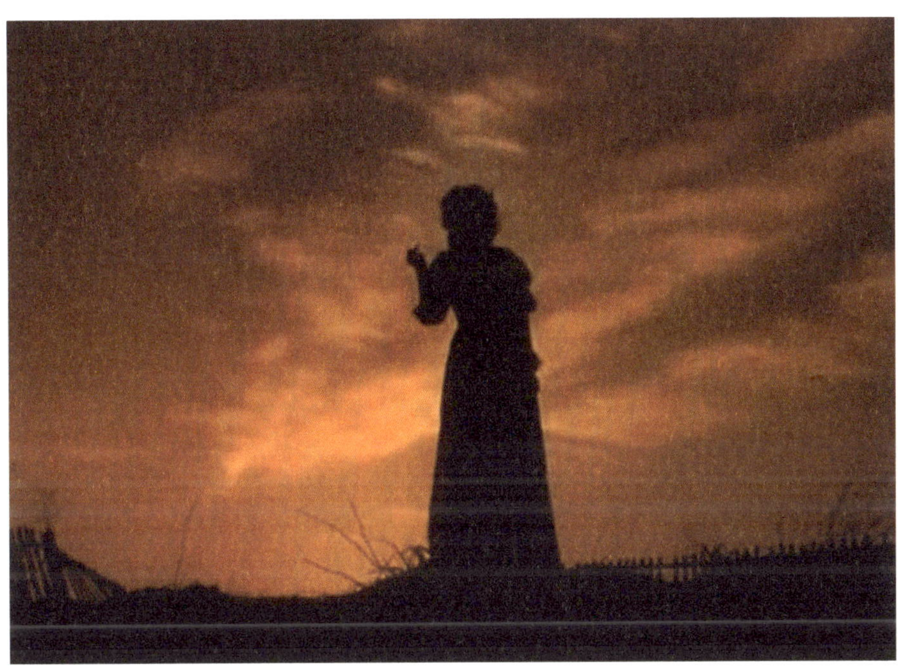

“As God is my witness, as God is my witness they’re not going to lick me. I’m going to live through this and when it’s all over, I’ll never be hungry again. No, nor any of my folk. If I have to lie, steal, cheat or kill. As God is my witness, I’ll never be hungry again!”

Vivien Leigh as Scarlett O’Hara in Victor Fleming’s *Gone with the Wind*, 1939 (still)

concerns. But looking at the artist's act of creation from her perspective is only one component of a far more complex interpretative process. A crucial second stage involves an analysis of the ways that works of art and distinct styles galvanize historical discourses of which the artist may or may not have been consciously aware when creating them. In his renowned essay "The Death of the Author,"[31] Roland Barthes conjectured that the more categorical author function had already replaced the individual writer, and he concluded that the important creative work was now the task of readers.

The situation, however, is far more complex and intertwined than even Barthes suspected. Authors and artists are not simply catalysts for activating firmly established conventions, as Barthes asserts, since they must be actively involved in the important initial semiotic work of gauging to what degree they can transform entrenched signs while still maintaining a modicum of intelligibility so that viewers can still read them. After they orient these signs to new uses, the complex process of reading through a multiplicity of cultural lenses is undertaken. The art—as opposed to the artist—then becomes the focus of a creative process of reading intent on demonstrating how specific works of art can significantly reorient established discourses and in turn be altered by them. In terms of my discussion of Kara Walker's panoramic cycles of cutouts, the second part of this twofold process involves looking specifically at her work and its potential broader historic contexts. I would like now to discuss her references to stereotypes, shadows, and minstrel shows as participants in historical discourses, which play the dual role of first informing her work and then being inflected by it.

Some of the most perceptive analyses of racially based stereotypes have been undertaken by humanities scholar

Sander Gilman in the introduction to his study *Difference and Pathology: Stereotypes of Sexuality, Race, and Madness*, which examines a nineteenth-century woman known as the Hottentot Black Venus, who was paraded before European and American audiences as an exotic biological specimen and an exaggerated form of sexuality and who, in addition, was used to reinforce a stereotypical view of Black female sexuality.[32]

In his discussion, Gilman recalls that the term *stereotype* originated in the late eighteenth century as the name for the reproductive process of obtaining identical pieces of type from papier-mâché molds. This technical classification was soon transformed into a figurative and highly pejorative means for categorizing distinct entities, including ethnic groups unable to break away from the pejorative qualifiers identifying them.[33] In his work, Gilman invokes Ferdinand de Saussure's theory of polarities, which asserts that artificial signs gain meaning and relevance through ongoing systems of difference, to provide a linguistic basis for the formation of negative stereotypes. According to Gilman's theory, cultures are able to discern and designate terms as well as people through oppositions that ultimately result in a given group's self-identity becoming the positive term of a polarity while designating some outside entity as the negative other.[34] The creation of identity through the subsequent derogation of some hypothetical "other" results in prejudicial and certainly racist views that can easily be ossified into stereotypes.[35] Although Gilman does not refer to tribal groups such as Comanches, who isolated themselves with the distinguished epithet "the people," thereby relegating all nontribal members to a subhuman category, such extreme jingoism provided the rationale for their brutality to outsiders. Such derogation of others has always been racism's standard fare; it remains a great challenge to achieve an equitable world.

Within the constraints of his argument, Gilman is extraordinarily lucid and to the point. Although he understands how racist stereotypes might develop from polarities, he does not venture into the even broader understanding of them as necessary concomitants to language, i.e., as forms of abstraction that equip people with sufficient generalities and biases to make communication possible. Gilman stops short of such a tactic when he states:

> All structured systems of representation, no matter what the medium, can be construed as "texts" for the study of stereotypes. . . . This is not to reduce the "work of art" to a system of stereotypical signifiers, but rather to stress that such systems are incorporated within the work of art, high or low, and shape the fictions that these works present.[36]

The concept of the stereotype as a necessary yet inadequate shorthand referring to elements in the world has a distinguished background going back to Plato's dialogue, the *Cratylus*. In this dialogue, Socrates demonstrates that words cannot be exact imitations of things because their primary function as signs distinguishes them from the objects they represent, thereby creating a space between the two. "The effect produced by the names upon things of which they are the names would be ridiculous, if they were to be entirely like them in every respect," Socrates argues, "for everything would be duplicated, and no one could tell in any case which was the real thing and which the name."[37] Referring to these signs (whether artistic representations or language) as "images," Socrates reminds us that a disparity between them and reality is necessary since the former are the indispensable abstractions that provide us with a foothold in the world and an ability to manipulate it even if only insufficiently. This necessary impoverishment of reality—equivalent to the symbolic realm's ability to encompass the Real that psychologist Jacques Lacan called *"objet petit a"*[38]—is equivalent to a stereotypical view of the world without attendant pejorative connotations. Thus, we can conclude that stereotypes might begin as neutral designations but only a significant few become the disparaging terms Gilman describes.

This brief excursion into the background of stereotypes, including their necessary aspects and prejudicial miens, enables us to consider Socrates's definition of language's essential abstraction in relation to Kara Walker's art. From the above discussion, it should be evident that, in addition to being criticisms of racist ideology, Walker's works are also ironic demonstrations of the inability of culture ever to come to terms with reality, since the Real must always be constituted in terms of available languages. By its very nature, culture is a construct; it is often understood in terms of words and/or signs, which, at the outset, are abstractions and conventions. All words used to characterize Blacks and whites as polarized racial types, for example, are inadequate handles—stereotypes, readily available containers or molds—that make the world manageable at the same time they impoverish it. Instead of considering stereotypes as "a universal means of coping with anxieties engendered by our inability to control the world,"[39] as Gilman attests, I suggest that they are in fact accepted, if inadequate, ways of dealing with it, even if they can lead us to the programmatic travesties of humanity that Harlequin and Silhouette romances espouse and Walker's work makes abundantly clear. The inability of conventional signs or stereotypes to be in sync with reality coupled with their lack of originality are among their most damning traits, but without them we would not have any common terms on which to agree.

Walker's work provides us with an understanding of stereotypes as conventional ways of representing the world and also as racist constructs. In her representations, both Blacks and whites collude with one another. According to her panoramas, their collusion is both an orgy of types and an impossible and often warped romance of signs that replaces and largely obviates the reality they are supposed to delineate.

In addition to playing with stereotypical figures arising from the antebellum South, Walker's art participates in a shadowy realm that deserves far greater explication than it has thus far been given in writings about her work. Shadows function as both indexes and icons, to use Charles S. Peirce's characterization of an index as a motivated and contingent sign and an icon as an illustrative one, since they are (1) dependent on an external light source directed toward a given entity and (2) representations of that same entity.[40] In a candid 1996 interview with the critic Jerry Saltz, Walker confirmed her knowledge of shadows' dual connections with the articles and beings they adumbrate:

> You find a silhouette in an antique store and you know that there's a person, a sitter, whose shadow this is. . . . Shadows, shadows of shadowy characters, shadows of artificial things, shadows of stereotypes, shadows of things that maybe there's only a written description of. . . . [My art] is silhouetting a fiction, the fiction of history; the fiction that has come out of history. We speak of history in odd terms. I sort of condensed it to the fictional—of romance fiction, or stories, books, novels, *Gone with the Wind*, *Uncle Tom's Cabin*. It's a genre, like the historical romance. . . . I had to make the silhouette because I think I could never really condense anything in painting form.[41]

Because shadows are metonyms associated with the forms they trace as well as representations of them, they have proven to be excellent devices for representing the birth of painting. The first account of this origination of this art form is contained in Pliny the Elder's *Natural History*.[42] An important Neoclassical retelling of it is found in a paper that Swiss artist Johann Heinrich Fuseli delivered to the Royal Academy of Arts in London. According to Fuseli:

> Greek painting took its first faltering steps, it was rocked in the cradle by the graces and taught to speak by Love. If ever a legend deserved to be believed it was the love story of the young Corinthian girl who with her secret lamp drew the outline of her lover's shadow just before his departure, thus provoking our sympathy to trust in it, and leading us to make a few observations on the first complex effort at painting, as well as on this linear method which seems to have remained the founding act long after the agent for whom it was primarily conceived had been forgotten. . . . The earliest experiments in this art were the *skia-grams*, simple outlines of shadows—similar to those which have been circulated amongst the common people by amateurs and other parasites of physiognomy under the name of silhouettes.[43]

Written in 1801, Fuseli's statement is a critical document for Neoclassical studies since it connects silhouettes directly with the origin of art and indirectly with the vogue for black-figure Greek vases that were then being discovered in Etruscan tombs. The young maiden in Pliny's account is Dibutades, the daughter of the Greek potter Butades, who filled her outline with clay and fired it with the rest of his pots in hopes that a more tangible representation would comfort her. In my estimation, the story of the departed lover's shadow as an inspiration for painting, together with its implication of his possible death, resonated with the Greco-Roman description of departed souls in Hades as "shades," so that the birth of art came to be associated with the death of its subject.

Such an estimation of art's function enables us to reconsider the shadowy silhouettes inhabiting Kara Walker's art. Their status as ideological constructs bespeaks not a double death but instead a twofold removal from life since the shades represented in her work are unable to die because their only prior existence is a fictive one. Instead of denoting the essence of an individual soul, Walker's shadows are extrinsic forms detached from humanity, which they only distantly resemble. Molds for replicating reality on a par with Andy Warhol's standardized products, her stereotypical shadows are both absences and voids. "It's a blank space," Walker said to Saltz in reference to her silhouettes, "but it's not at all a blank space, it's both there and not there."[44] Her images are similar to the likenesses presented to the hypothetical prisoners in Plato's cave, whose only sense of reality are the pale vestiges of Forms in the guise of shadows, which could be construed, as they are in Walker's art, as ideological constructs. Unlike the shadows described by the psychologist C. G. Jung that are purported to represent the essence of an individual's repressed self or a collective identity pleading for recognition, Walker's shades are far from repressed: instead of begging for acknowledgment, they are blatantly disruptive in their attempts to supplant reality through shock.

Fuseli's reference to the origins of painting coupled with his objection to "other parasites of physiognomy under the name of silhouettes" points to the now-discredited science of physiognomy promoted by his fellow countryman and close friend, the minister Johann Kaspar Lavater (1741–1801). In its overweening emphasis on the cranium and related cartilaginous areas, physiognomy differs from pathognomy, which purports to explicate the meaning of facial expressions created by coordinated movements of muscle and skin. In her interview with Saltz, Walker indicated her knowledge of Lavater's physiognomy when she pointed to the nineteenth-century vogue for silhouettes and their connection with it:

> [The silhouette tradition] comes from a sort of polite middle-class society to some extent. It's not as haughty and aristocratic as a full-fledged oil painting portrait. Everyone could get one for a few pennies—and you had image, you had connection with physiognomy.[45]

There is little doubt that the late eighteenth- and early nineteenth-century fashion for silhouettes developed from Lavater's tremendously popular demonstrations of physiognomy's merits published in his *Physiognomische Fragmente zur Beförderung der Menschenkenntnis und Menschenliebe* (four volumes, 1775–78) and its English version, *Essays on Physiognomy* (1789–98). By 1810, fifty-five editions of Lavater's works had been printed, twenty of them in England alone. The first American edition of Lavater's work was published in 1794 in Boston. Six years later a condensed version, *The Pocket Lavater*, was printed. No less significant a figure than Johann Wolfgang von Goethe (1749–1832) helped Lavater with his book. Their close friendship ended, however, when Goethe lost respect for Lavater's compulsion to convert people to his way of thinking, which he came to revere almost as if it were a new religion.

There is admittedly an intense spiritual subtext to Lavater's physiognomy since it developed out of the mystical thought of Emanuel Swedenborg (1688–1772). In particular, it relies on Swedenborg's idealist view of the world as a revelation of God's essential being through His creations so that distinct correspondences between spiritual and earthly realms are evident as well as those separating the interior realms and exterior visages of human beings. Taking up Swedenborg's theory, Lavater posited the concept of silhouettes as the primary diagnostic tool for physiognomic studies, since he assumed that the divine spirit had a definite impact on human features. In Platonic terms, the profile was considered to be closer to the level of ultimate Forms than the incidental accidents of symmetry or its lack, since it was credited with reflecting formative psychic energies.[46]

Lavater is guilty of subscribing to such clichés as aristocratic high foreheads, brutish thick lips, and determined jaws, indicating his role as a synthesizer of popular attitudes rather than a discoverer of a new interpretative tool. Even so, his *Essays on Physiognomy*, detailing sets of profiles together with his descriptions of how they reveal predominant individual features, influenced many painters. It also stimulated the widespread fashion for silhouettes, named derisively for Étienne de Silhouette (1709–67), the French finance minister under Louis XV who was notorious for being stingy and who had made cut shadow portraits as a hobby. The phrase *à la silhouette* came to connote extreme penuriousness, and the word *silhouette* was consequently used to refer to a modest means for achieving convincing likeness by cutting an array of portraits and scenes from paper quickly and easily. Even though silhouettes were made before Lavater, his purported diagnostic of using them to reveal God's great repository of molds—those unalterable and unquestionable character traits appearing in the profiles of his sitters—made them highly prized forms of portraiture.

Lavater's work may have received great popular acclaim, but as early as the 1780s it was being regarded as suspect by serious thinkers. With hindsight, his most important legacy appears to be not the verifiability of his system, which can in no way be substantiated, but his ability to create and set in action the basic terms of a new discourse on profiles in general and shadows in particular that enabled Romantics to look at them as indices of a distinct form of intelligibility.

In the early nineteenth century, shadows began to slough off their secondary status of dependency and assume a new primary role. One of the first important texts to take up this theme was Adelbert von Chamisso's 1813 novella of Peter Schlemihl's Faustian agreement to sell his shadow to the Devil in return for unlimited wealth.[47] In this story, von Chamisso relies on Lavater's equation of shadows with essences even though he differs from the Swiss thinker in terms of leaving this tale's ultimate meaning unsettled. Although Schlemihl's shadow in this story is presented as a passive appendage whose paramount importance is only recognized by its absence, its significance changes with the circumstances in which the protagonist finds himself. Von Chamisso's account provides us with ample justification to think of the departed shadow as an unacknowledged conscience or as an open-ended reflection of Schlemihl's destabilized character that is out of sync with the established Biedermeier world in which he lived.

Several decades after von Chamisso's story, the famous Danish fairy-tale writer, Hans Christian Andersen, who was known among his close associates for his charming way of entertaining their children with spontaneous cut-outs of dancers, swans, castles, and fantastic figures, wrote an entirely different type of morality tale entitled "The Shadow."[48] This story updates von Chamisso's characterization of a shadow by attributing new independence to it.

Anderson alludes to a racist subtext for this former appendage's new sovereignty when he situates the opening scenes in a southern region where "the sun can burn properly," and notes, with half-hearted wonder, that "people [in these regions] become as brown as mahogany all over; in the very hottest countries they are even burnt into Negroes."[49] In this atmosphere the Shadow is emboldened to desert the learned man to whom he had been attached. Years later, he returns to this former master to recount the adventures and wealth his self-proclaimed autonomy had brought him, noting, "I've become so much of a body that I've actually got flesh and clothes; you never expected to see me in such fine condition."[50] The Shadow then invites the learned man to be his traveling companion, and suggests a change in roles in which his former master would now become his shadow. When the learned man asks if he might use the familiar pronoun *thou* when addressing the Shadow, the latter demurs:

> Now I get just that sensation when I hear you say "thou" to me. I feel absolutely as if I were crushed down on the ground, as I was in my first situation with you. You understand, it's merely a sensation, not pride at all. I can't bear you saying "thou" to me, but I'll gladly say "thou" to you; and that's meeting you halfway."[51]

In order to explain the three-dimensional presence of his former master who now plays the subsidiary role of his shadow, the Shadow asks the Princess, whom he is courting:

> Do you see the person who always goes about with me? Other people have an ordinary shadow, but I don't care about what is ordinary. You give your servant finer clothes for his livery than you wear yourself, and just so I have had my shadow smartened up into a man. What's more, you can

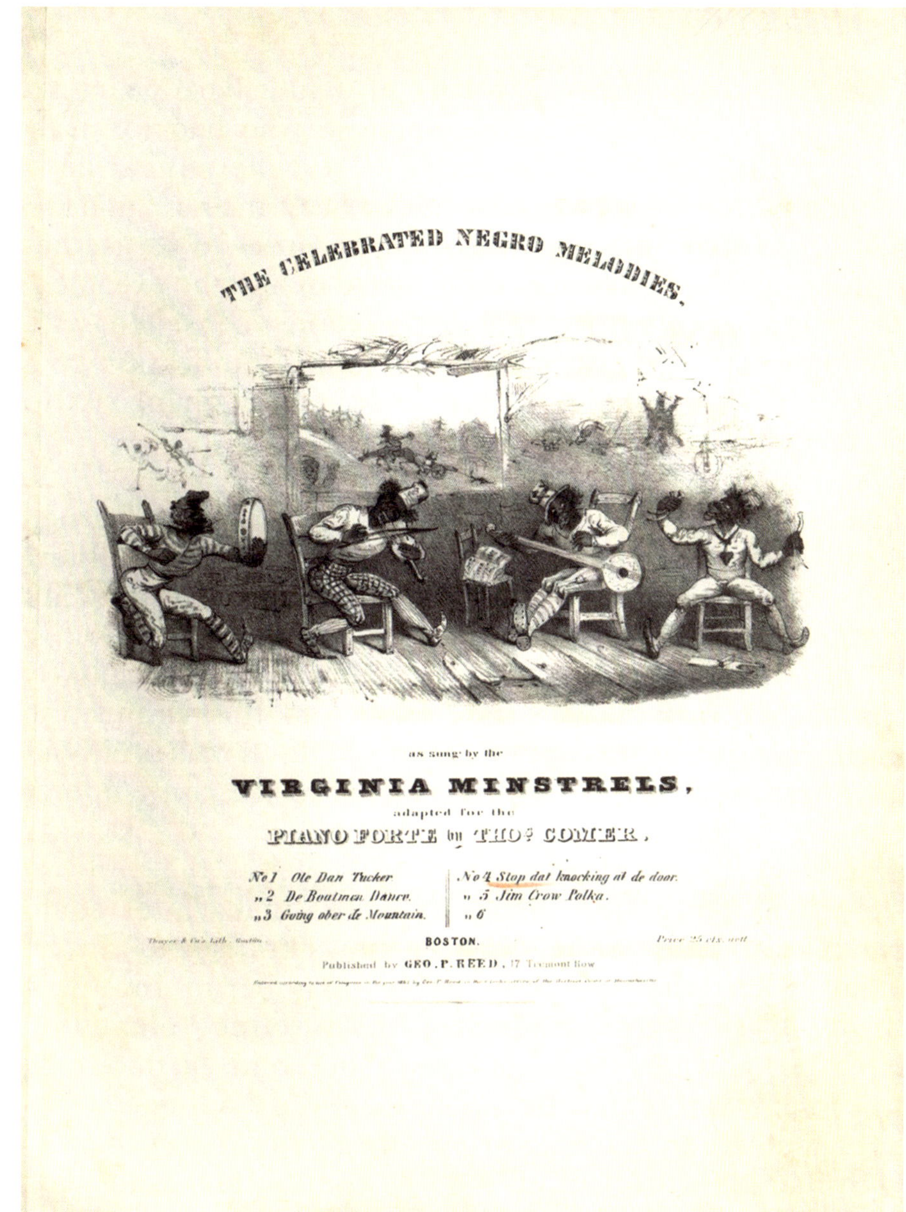


Cover, *The Celebrated Negro Melodies, as Sung by the Virginia Minstrels*, c. 1843

> see that I have even given him a shadow. It costs money, but I do like to have something peculiar to myself."[52]

Later, in a role reversal worthy of Baudrillard's simulation, the Shadow accuses his shadow, who had formerly been his master, of going insane. "He believes that he is the man," the Shadow exclaims to the Princess, "and I—just think of it—am his shadow."[53] In order to please her suitor, the Princess orders the learned man to be executed. The moral of this story—a lesson certainly consistent with Walker's art—is that the Shadow, the personification of a stereotype, ultimately kills off the humanity giving rise to it and installs itself as ruling sovereign.

The detachment of Andersen's Shadow from the learned man is as significant as it is threatening. Its implied subtext links it to Blacks, who were perceived as potentially dangerous if they achieved autonomy. In the United States, for example, wanted posters for runaway slaves regularly characterized them as silhouettes. And this connection between runaway slaves and errant shadows makes silhouettes in general an intriguing parallel to the contemporaneous development of the hugely popular and distinctly American theatrical phenomenon known as the minstrel show, which presents Blacks as masks that whites could colonize and lampoon. Minstrel shows first started in the 1820s when working-class white men began inventing wildly exaggerated parodies of the carefree "plantation Negro," known as the "Jim Crow type," and the dandified freedman, who they called "Zip Coon." In doing so, they helped devise the racist conventions of the "happy darky" with bulging eyes, gaping mouth, and big feet who liked to sleep, fish, dance, and eat possum or coon, and who spoke a butchered form of English notable for its mispronunciations and malapropisms. Not just a middlebrow

## Slaves–Slaves.

The subscriber has just received and offers for sale at his old stand, No. 7 Moreau street, Third Municipality, New Orleans, the largest lot of NEGROES in the city, consisting of house servants, field hands, and mechanics. They will be sold on reasonable terms for cash or good paper. [mh9—2m] WM. F. TALBOTT

---

TWENTY-FIVE DOLLARS REWARD—Will be paid for the apprehension of the mulatto boy DANIEL, aged about twenty three years and about five feet five inches high. He left his master's plantation in Iberville on the evening of the 9th inst., and came to this city on the steamboat E. D. White. The above reward will be paid for his delivery at the parish jail, or to W. M. GREENWOOD,

mh16—6t 40 Old Levee street.

---

TWENTY-FIVE DOLLARS REWARD—Ran away in the early part of February, the negro man RINGGOLD. He is about 34 years old, about 5 feet 3 or 4 inches high; is a griff; can speak a little French; is a carpenter, whitewasher, &c. The public are cautioned against employing or harboring said boy. Any person delivering the said boy to me at McDonoghville, shall receive the above reward.

mh18—8t* CHARLES KORNER.

---

TEN DOLLARS REWARD—Ran away on the 15th January, my negro woman ROSETTA, black, 36 years of age, 5 feet 5 or 6 inches high. She belongs to the estate of Mr. Isaac Pipkin, deceased. I will give the above reward to any one who will apprehend and deliver her up at Warwick & Martin's trading yard, Common street.

mh18—tf W. B. MUSE, agent for the heirs.

---

TWENNTY DOLLARS REWARD—Ran away on the 6th inst., from the plantation of A. Armitage, on Bayou Lafourche, the negro man JOE, about 40 years of age, 5 feet 6 inches high, dark griffe very stout and broad shouldered, heavy dull manner and a husky voice when speaking, has a sore on his left shin bone not yet quite well. He is in all probability to be found about the steamboats, having been hired by his former owner, Capt. D. Kinney, as a fireman on the tow boats. We will give the above reward to any one arresting him and putting him in jail, and advising us of the same.

mh18—10t CAMMACK & SQUIRES.

Advertisements announcing a slave auction and rewards for the return of runaway slaves, *The Daily Picayune* (New Orleans), March 20, 1852

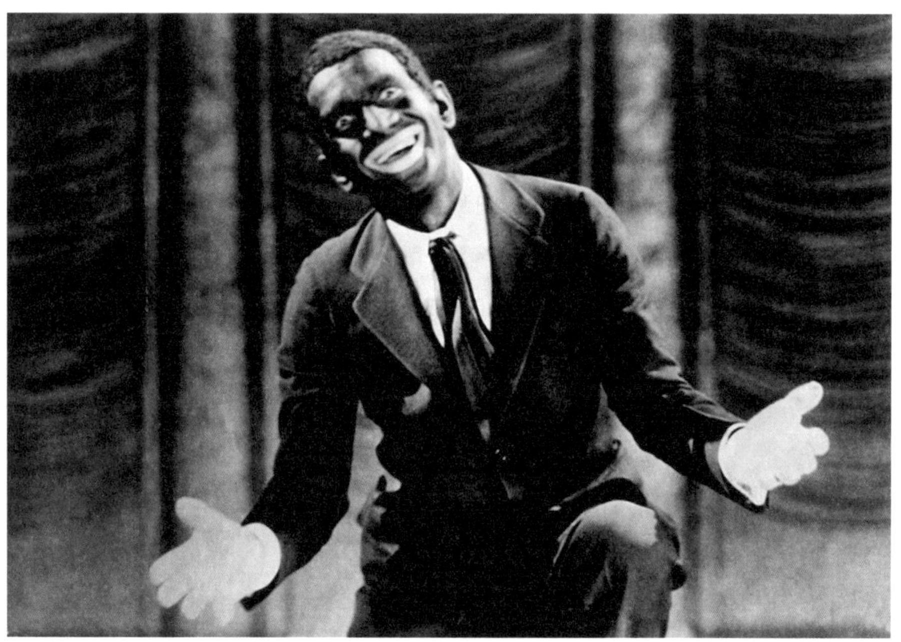

Al Jolson singing "Mammy" in *The Jazz Singer,* 1927 (still)

or lowbrow entertainment, minstrel shows attracted the attention of such luminaries as Abraham Lincoln, William Ewart Gladstone, and William Makepeace Thackeray, among others. Harriet Beecher Stowe's famous antislavery novel *Uncle Tom's Cabin* appears to have been influenced by minstrel shows and in turn had an impact on them when it became the basis for a popular full-length minstrel play. Since this nineteenth-century genre permitted otherwise censorious racist remarks to be baldly stated as humorous quips, it is no coincidence that its incredible popularity paralleled the abolitionist, Civil War, and Reconstruction eras. During those times, issues of race were vehemently debated, and Blacks, whose rights were regularly abused, became the object of concerted derision.

Although the minstrel show might appear far removed from the present, many of its songs, including "My Old Kentucky Home," "Oh! Sussana," and "Carry Me Back to Old Virginny" are still well known today. And neo-minstrelsy over the years has taken many forms, including Al Jolson's blackface routines in *The Jazz Singer*; Elvis Presley's early dancing, which so alarmed television censors he could only be filmed from the waist up; Little Richard's histrionics; television sitcoms such as *Amos 'n' Andy*, *Sanford and Son*, and *The Jeffersons*; Eddie Murphy's many voices; Ted Danson's 1993 appearance in blackface; and gangsta rap music videos.

In traditional minstrel shows, when whites appear in blackface, audiences can easily follow the actors' cues. They know exactly when to laugh and the humor is simple and straightforward, if brutal. The situation, however, began to change when Blacks themselves appeared in blackface. They not only had to wear the standard black curly wigs and appear in regulation burnt cork and lampblack with fire-engine-red exaggerated lips, but they also had to compete with white minstrel actors by imitating even their most outrageous caricatures. Although white audiences at first did not seem to look any further than the masks presented to them, the Black abolitionist Frederick Douglass, cited in the epigraph, was shocked and disapproving. In addition to humiliating Blacks, the presentation of African Americans in blackface conferred legitimacy on minstrelsy by implying that these images are self-delineated representations.[54] When one realizes that advertisements for slave auctions and the return of runaway slaves featured silhouettes, the irony of African Americans appearing in blackface in minstrel shows is definitely heightened.

Blacks' impersonation of whites in blackface constituted a Byzantine layering of images. Given this sequencing of impersonations and alienating identities, it may seem surprising that Black performers appeared so completely complicit with these theatrical displays that they contributed songs glorifying the Old South and making fun of their own subjugation. Recent research indicates that the Confederate anthem "Dixie" was composed by the Black musicians Ben and Lew Snowden, rather than the white minstrel Dan Emmett who helped make it famous.[55] And the Black minstrel performer Ernest Hogan wrote one of the most famous "coon songs," entitled "All Coons Look Alike to Me." While such collusion might seem egregious from our vantage point, the situation was obviously less clearly defined in the nineteenth century even though we can only imagine that such complicity was attained at an enormous cost. One only hopes that such participation created occasions for covert and insurrectionist signifying, but such innuendoes require pertinent contemporary observations in order to be substantiated and convincing ones have not yet come to light.

Instead of condemning these infractions, recent African American artists have perceived in these strata of

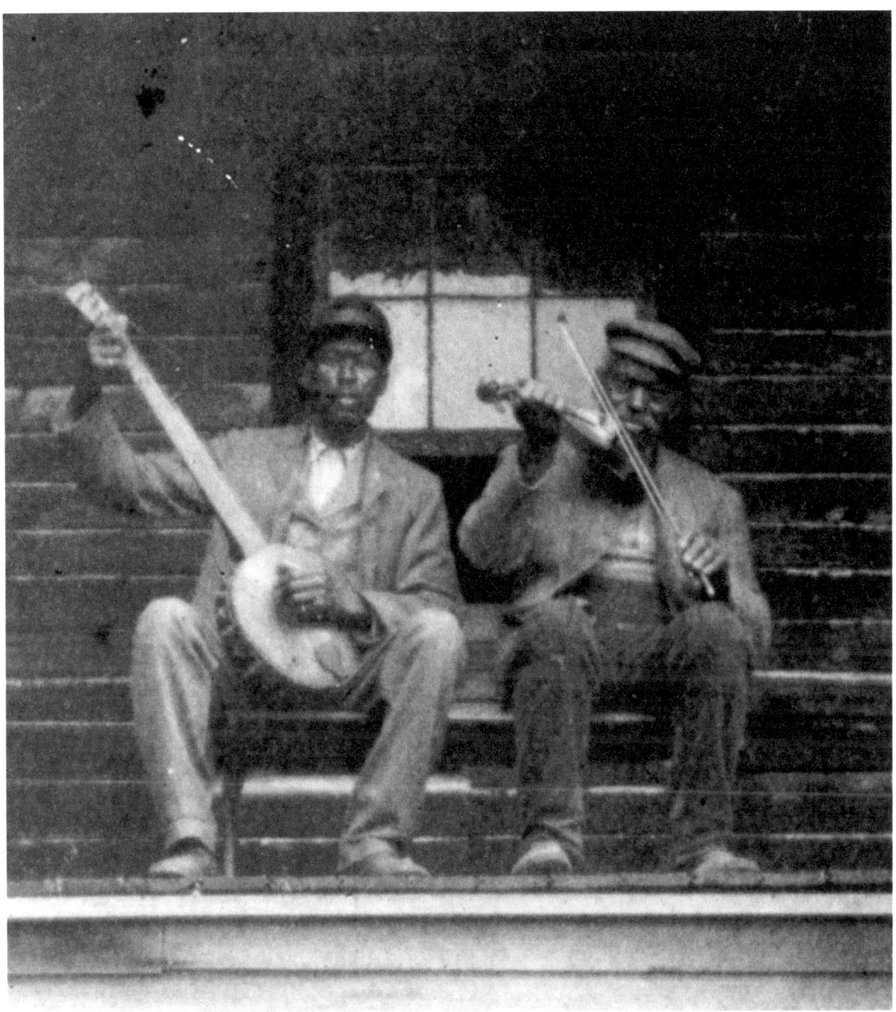

Ben and Lew Snowden, Clinton, Knox County, Ohio, c. 1890

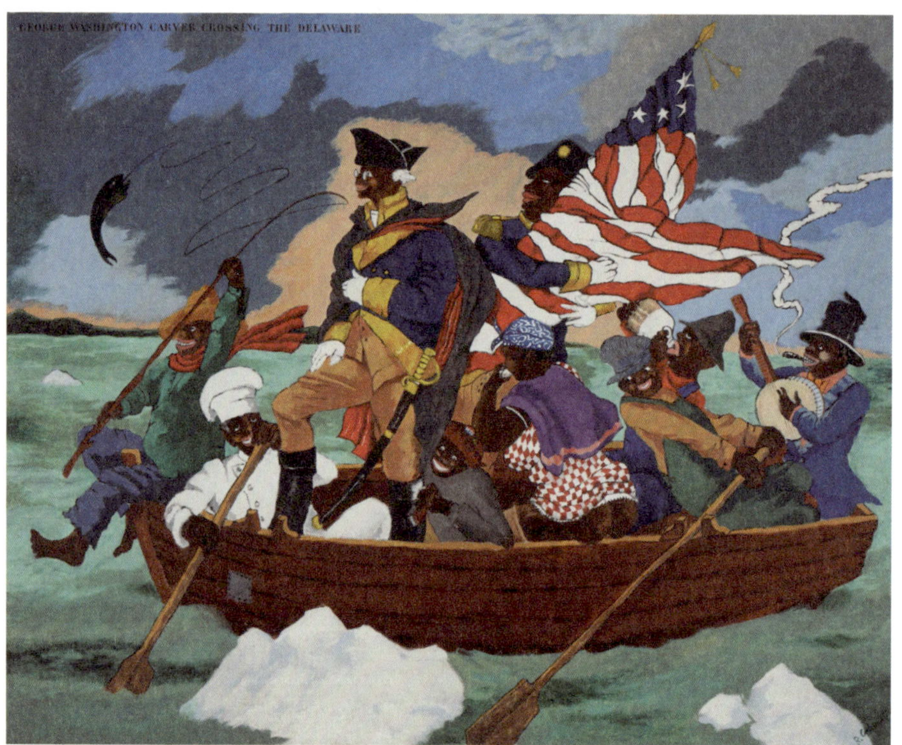


Robert Colescott, *George Washington Carver Crossing the Delaware, Page from an American History Textbook*, 1975, acrylic on canvas, 78½ × 98¼ inches (199.4 × 249.6 cm). Collection of the Lucas Museum of Narrative Art

imitations a pre-postmodern condition that dramatizes the ways in which types of mediation can be laminated onto one another. Robert Colescott's parodies are representative of the first postmodern generation's reaction to this material. In such pieces as *Eat Dem Taters* (1975) and *George Washington Carver Crossing the Delaware: Page from an American History Textbook* (also 1975), the artist appropriates works by Vincent van Gogh and Emanuel Leutze respectively. Rather than carrying out the multiple layers of masking that occurs in the nineteenth century when Blacks appear in blackface, Colescott signifies on the more straightforward minstrel shows so that the white figures appearing in the original paintings merge with their black masks to become cartooned visions of both Blacks and themselves. Because the joke is an insider prank, inclusive of both Blacks and whites, that is, enacted with good humor and sarcasm assuming the benignity of wit, it has upset few people. Its anachronistic formats cue viewers immediately into its retrospective view that reflects on how bad racial situations were in the past. With tongue firmly in cheek, it implies conditions are much better today.

Among her other tactics, Walker signifies on Colescott and the minstrel tradition. In her work, she "exaggerate[s] the exaggerations" that Frederick Douglass described in 1849 and reenacts the masking of Blacks in blackface, which has the cumulative effect of placing these stereotypes in even higher relief.[56] To them she adds the additional masquerade created by white shadows in blackface to demonstrate the wide-ranging authority of our dominant ideologies that mediate our present as well as our past and provide us with seemingly trivial escape routes such as Harlequin and Silhouette romances that are actually user-friendly prisons. It is no wonder that Walker's work has caused so much consternation in the Black community in the United States, where it became the subject of fierce debates in 1998 and the reason for a concerted letter-writing campaign, orchestrated by the African American artists Betye Saar and Howardena Pindell, protesting the so-called genius award conferred on her by the MacArthur Foundation. In view of the outrage surrounding this work, it is surprising how easily whites have accepted this art that lampoons ways that racist ideologies have also coerced and transformed them. Walker has attempted to turn a somewhat jaundiced eye on her popularity among white collectors since it has left her open to criticism from Blacks, who have accused her of playing to this audience. She confessed to *New York Times* critic Julia Szabo, "after a while I feel a bit like . . . Stepin Fetchit."[57]

In conclusion, I have hopefully indicated how connections between silhouettes and stereotypical images of African Americans depend on the link provided by the minstrel show. Consisting of ribald lampoons by actors called "delineators"—the theatrical equivalent to silhouettists—this entertainment parodied the veracity of Lavater's theories, which were still being evoked by silhouettes, at the same time that it used this residual truth claim to validate its negative view of Blacks. The world of the minstrel show was a mediated realm predicated on whites' outrageous satires of downtrodden Blacks. It did not matter if these white shadows in blackface were true or not; the important thing was that they were entertaining. And entertainment in turn gave truth to the lie these shows perpetuated. Building on the constructed nature of reality and the minstrel show's contribution to it, Walker's work uses this bowdlerized theatrical tradition as a lens for viewing the more widespread mass-mediated world in which we live. Her art overlays minstrelsy's feigned identities with the artificiality of the Harlequin antebellum romance to characterize the simulated and shadowy world many have continued to claim as real.

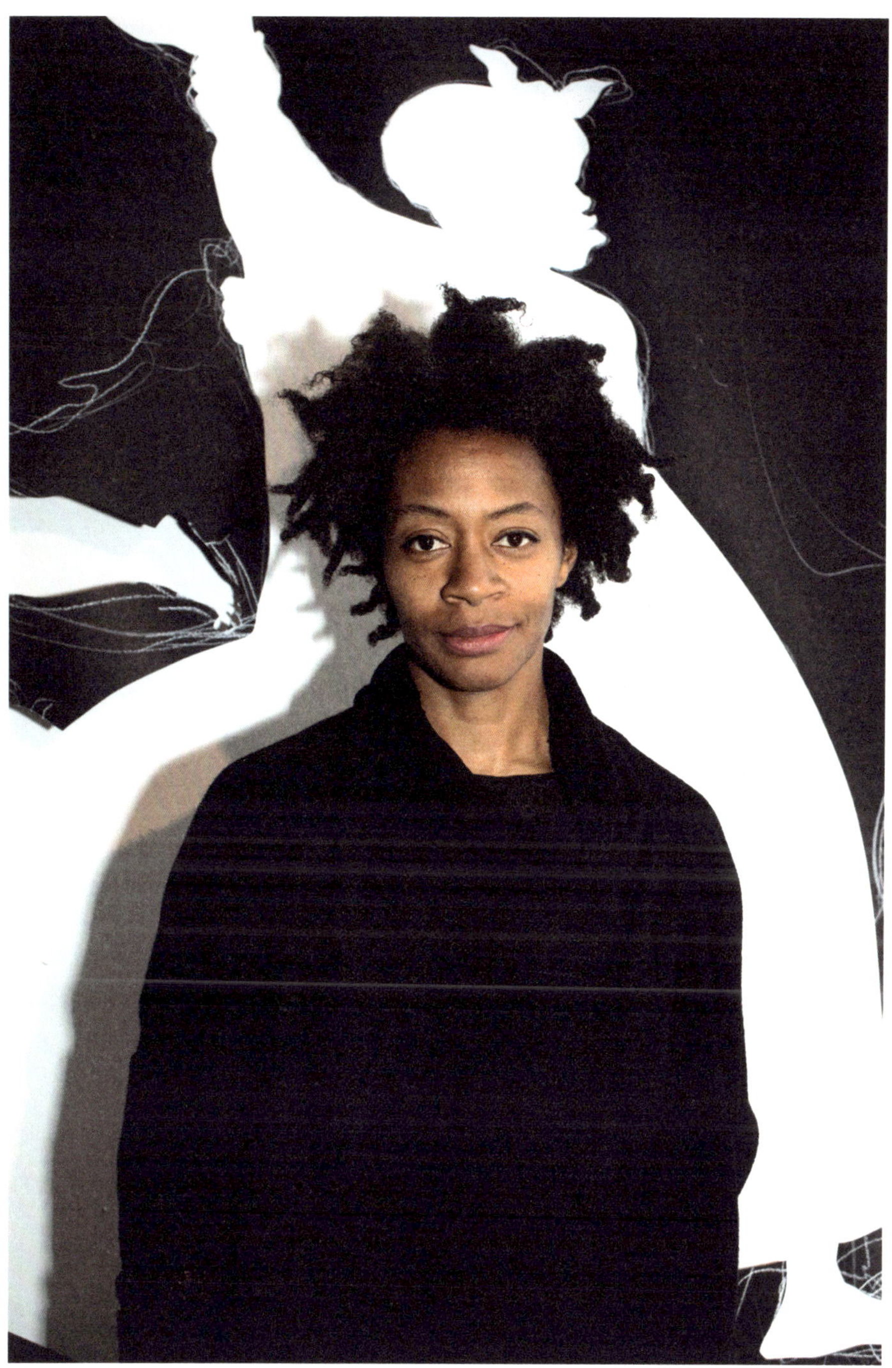

Kara Walker, 2018. Photo: Ari Marcopoulos

Kara Walker, *The End of Uncle Tom and the Grand Allegorical Tableau of Eva in Heaven*, 1995, cut paper and adhesive on wall, dimensions variable

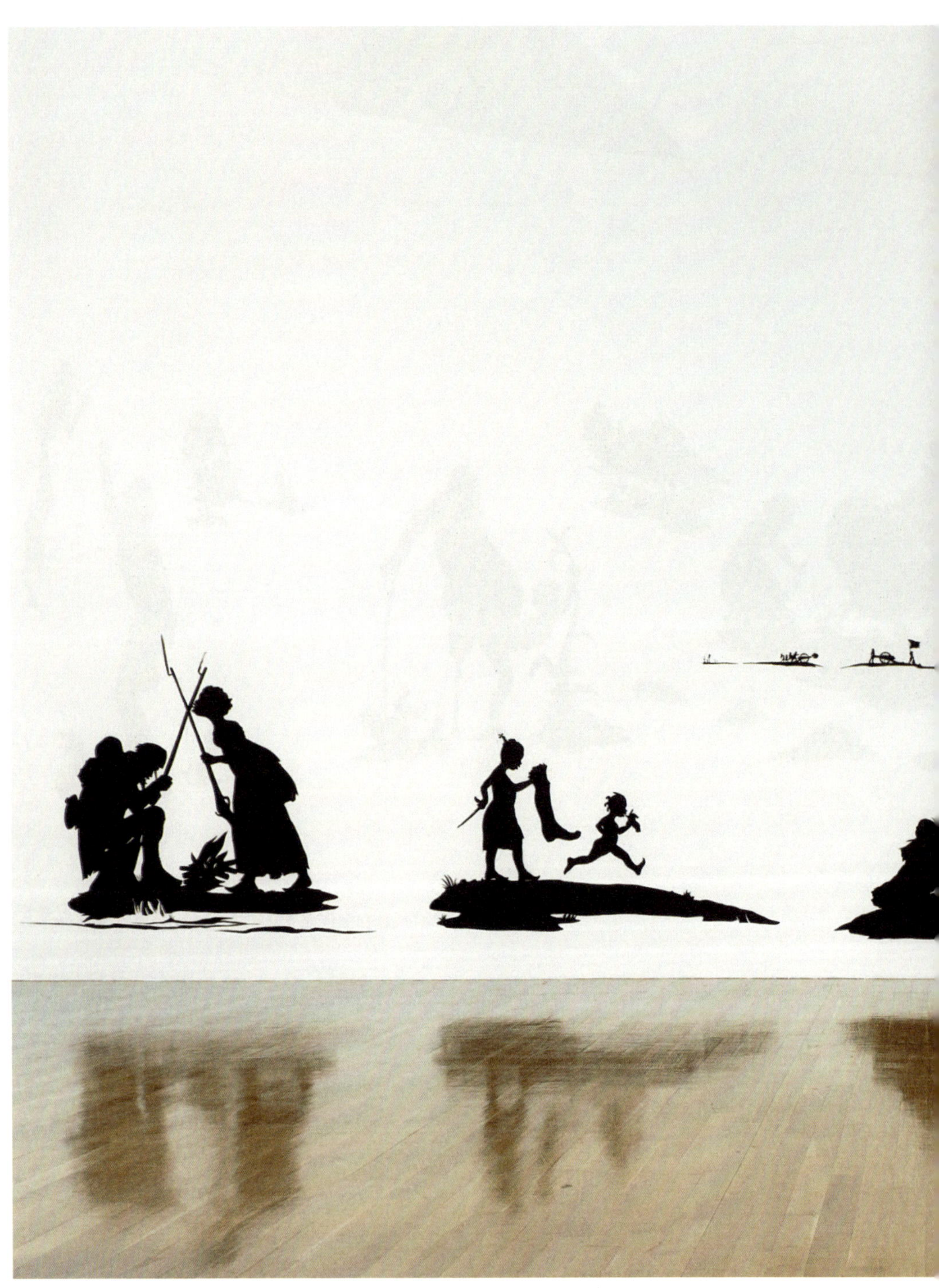

Kara Walker, *The Battle of Atlanta: Being the Narrative of a Negress in the Flames of Desire—A Reconstruction*, 1995, cut paper and adhesive on wall, 144 × 432 inches (365.8 × 1,097.3 cm). Collection of the Hammer Museum, Los Angeles

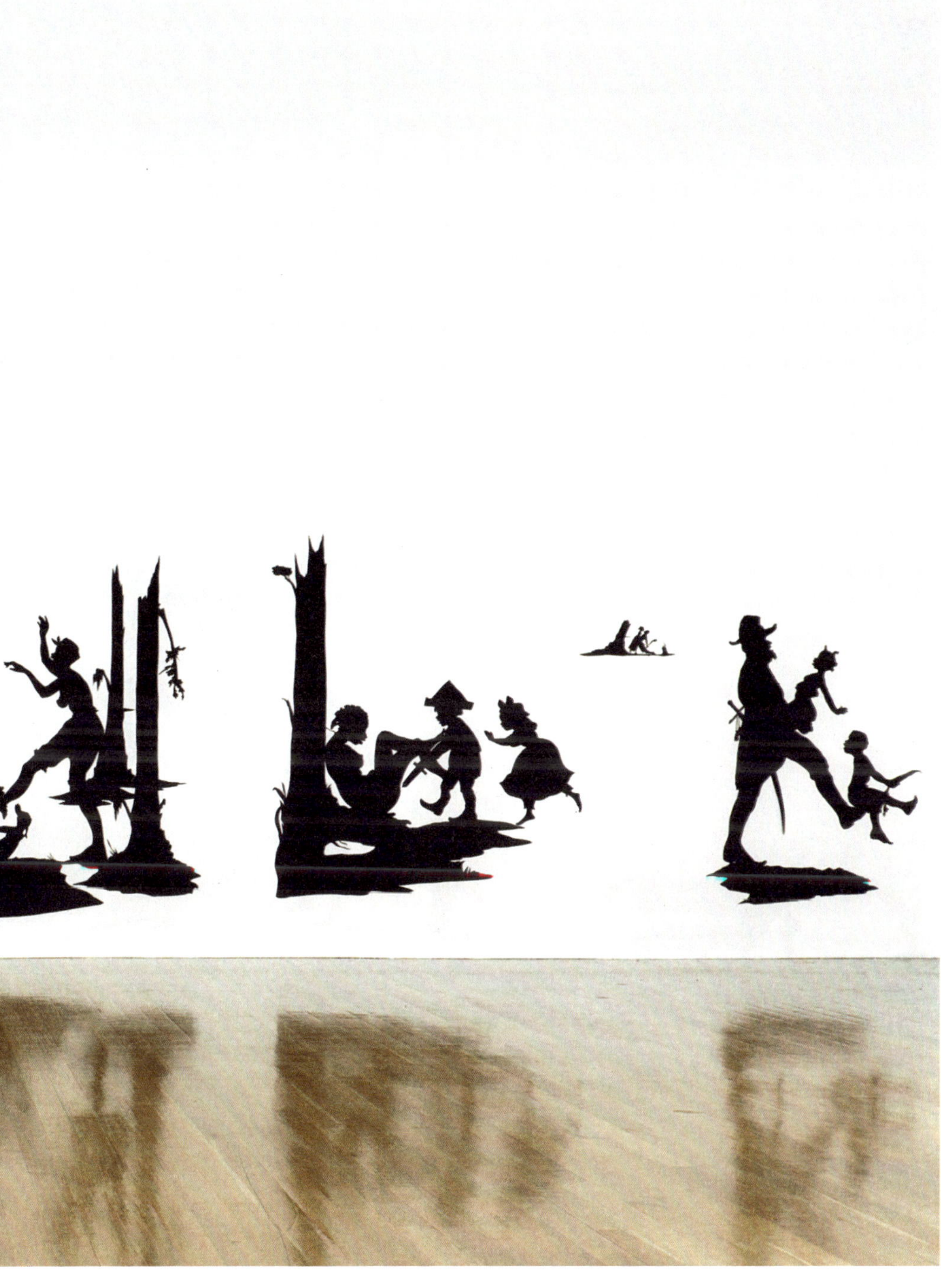

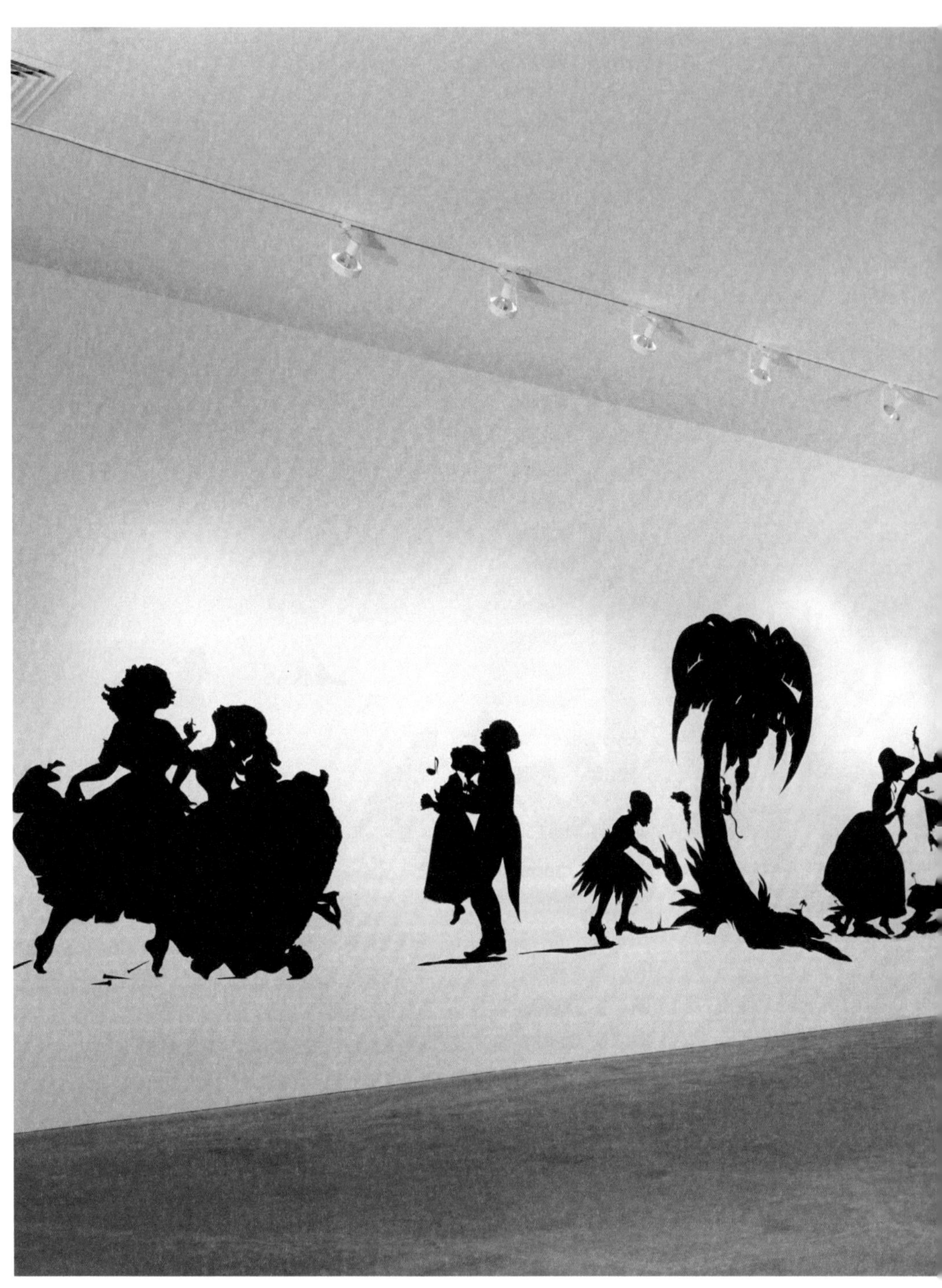

Kara Walker, *African't* (detail), 1996, cut paper and adhesive on wall, dimensions variable. Collection of The Broad, Los Angeles. Photo: Herbert Lotz

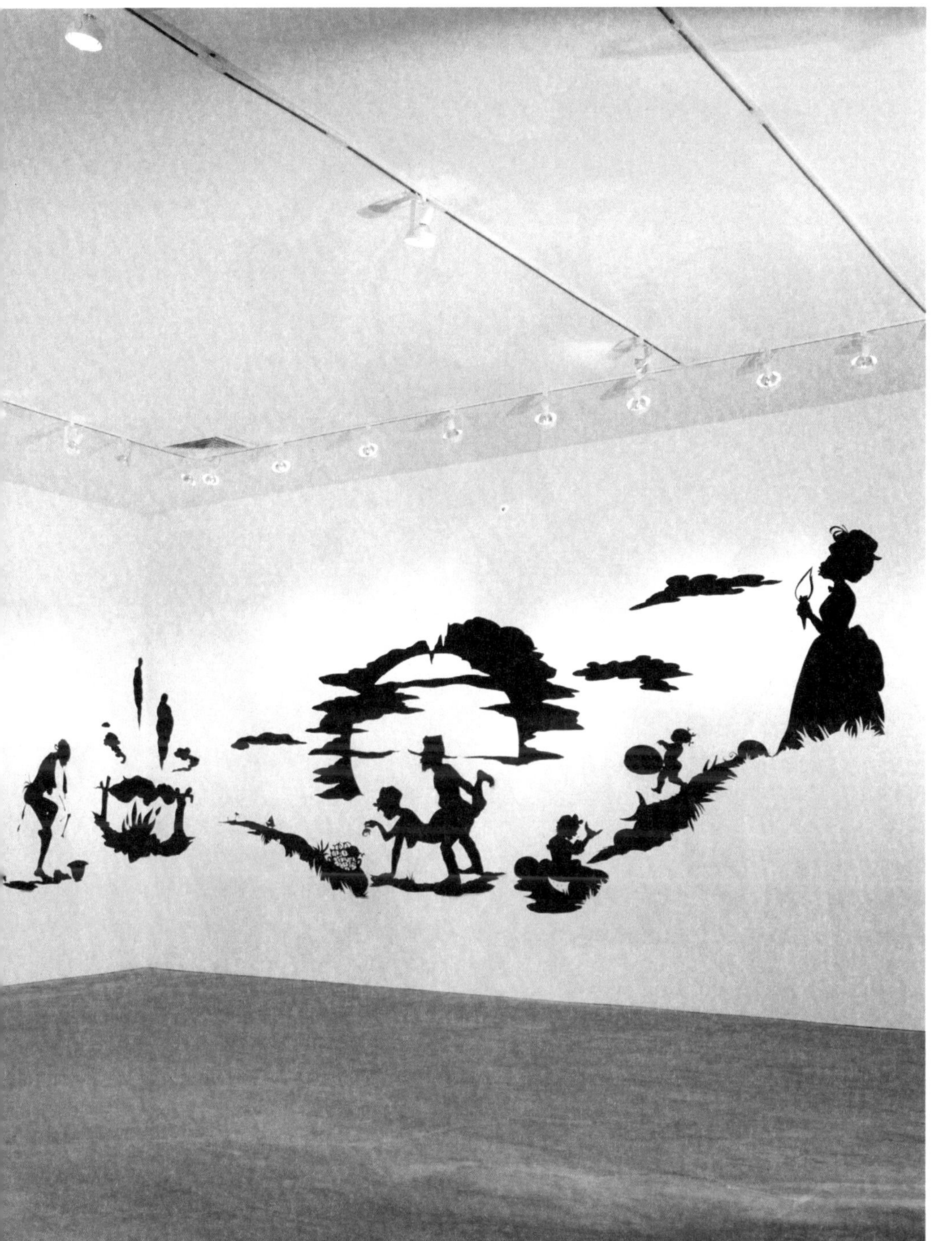

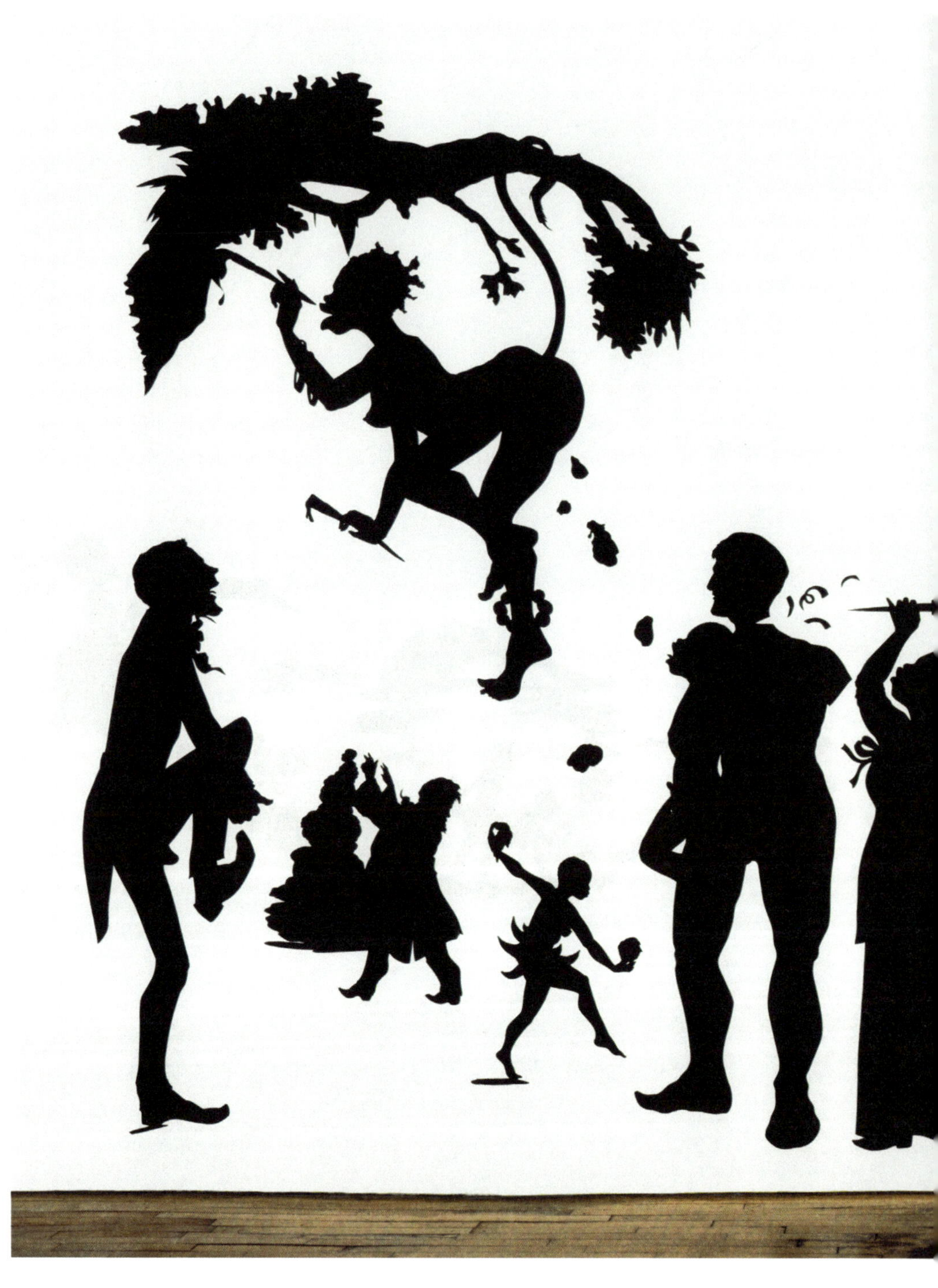

Kara Walker, *World's Exposition*, 1997, cut paper and adhesive on wall, dimensions variable

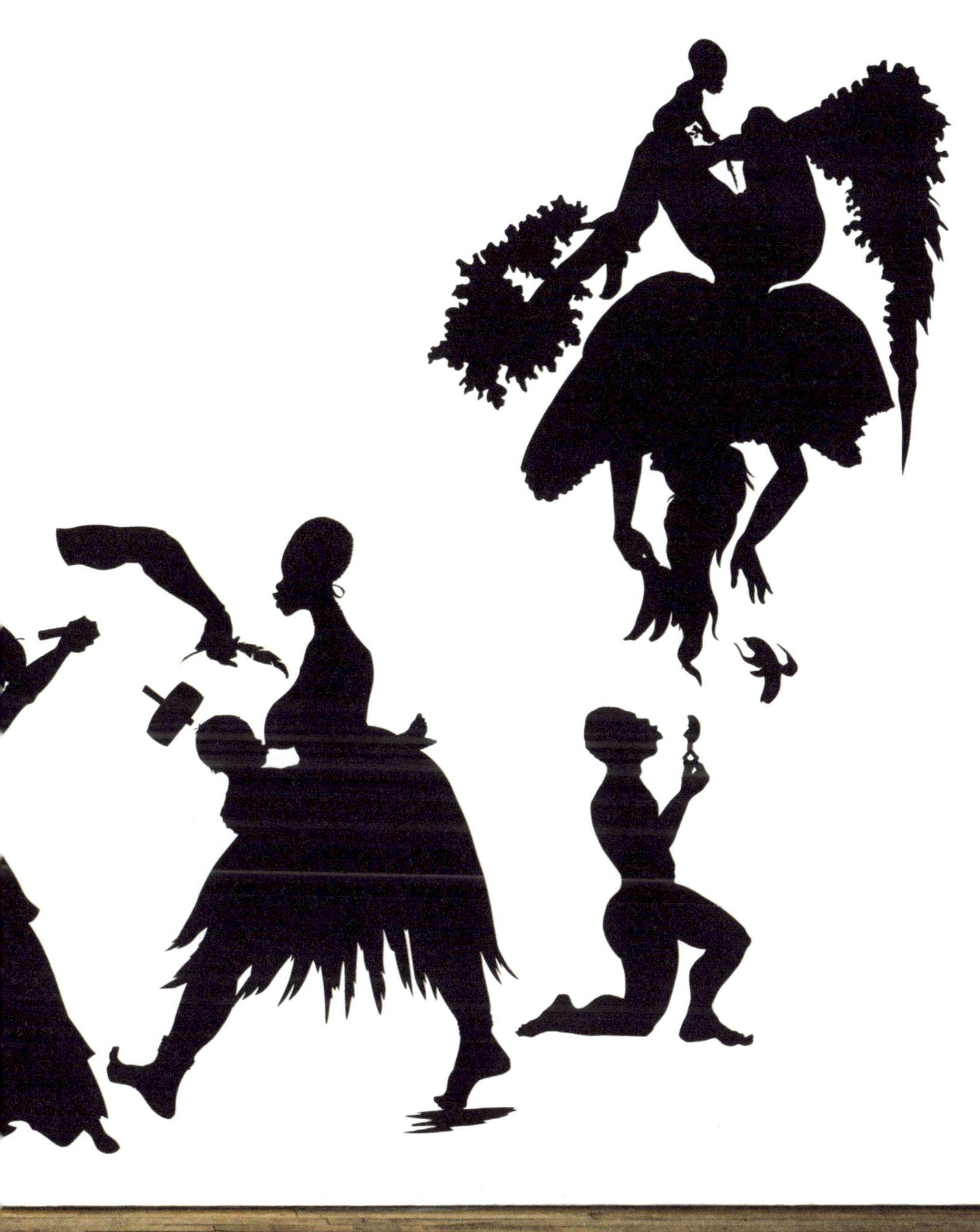

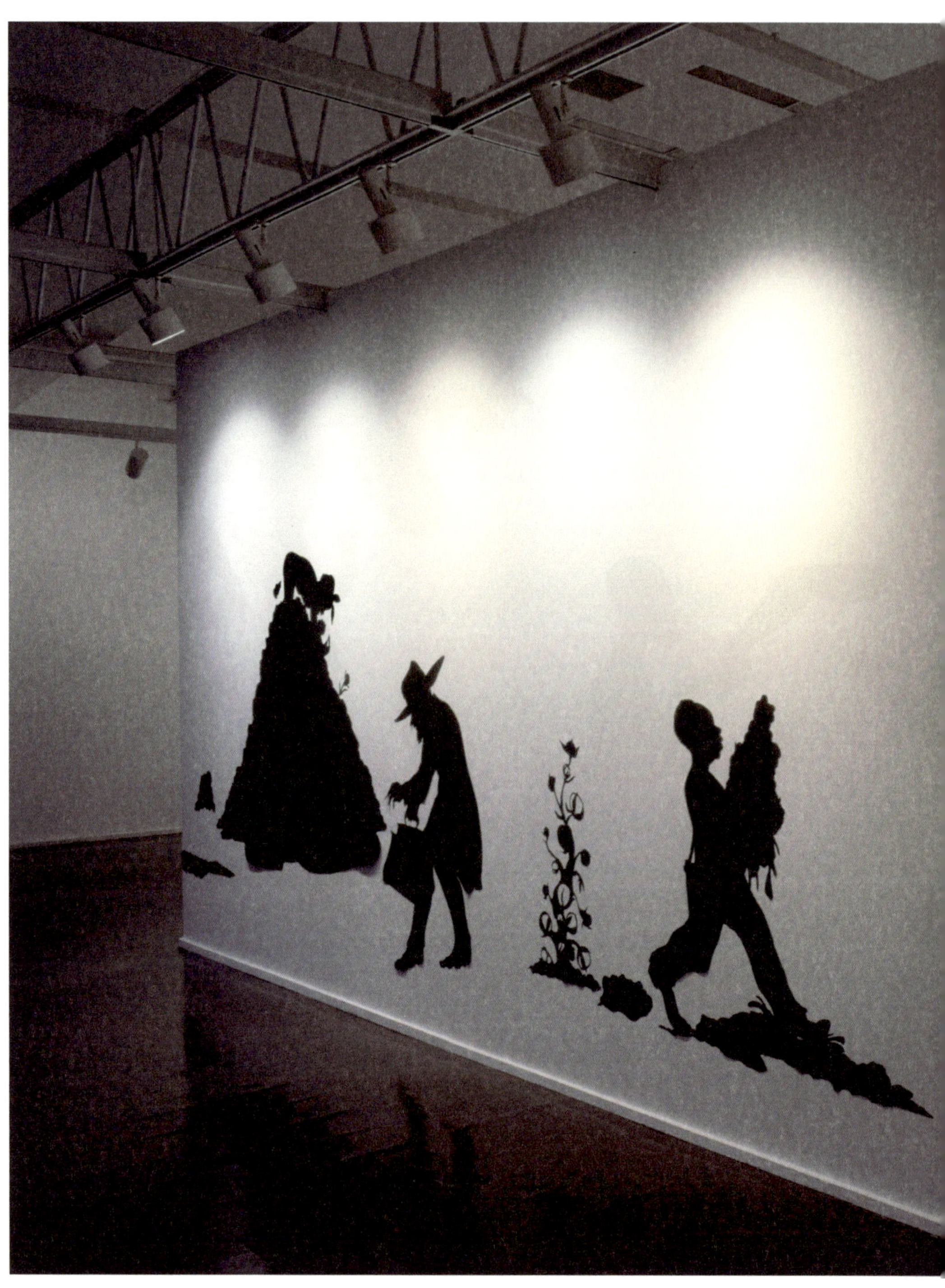

Pages 154–59: Kara Walker, *Presenting Negro Scenes Drawn Upon My Passage through the South and Reconfigured for the Benefit of Enlightened Audiences Wherever Such May Be Found, By Myself, Missus K. E. B. Walker, Colored* (details), 1997, cut paper and

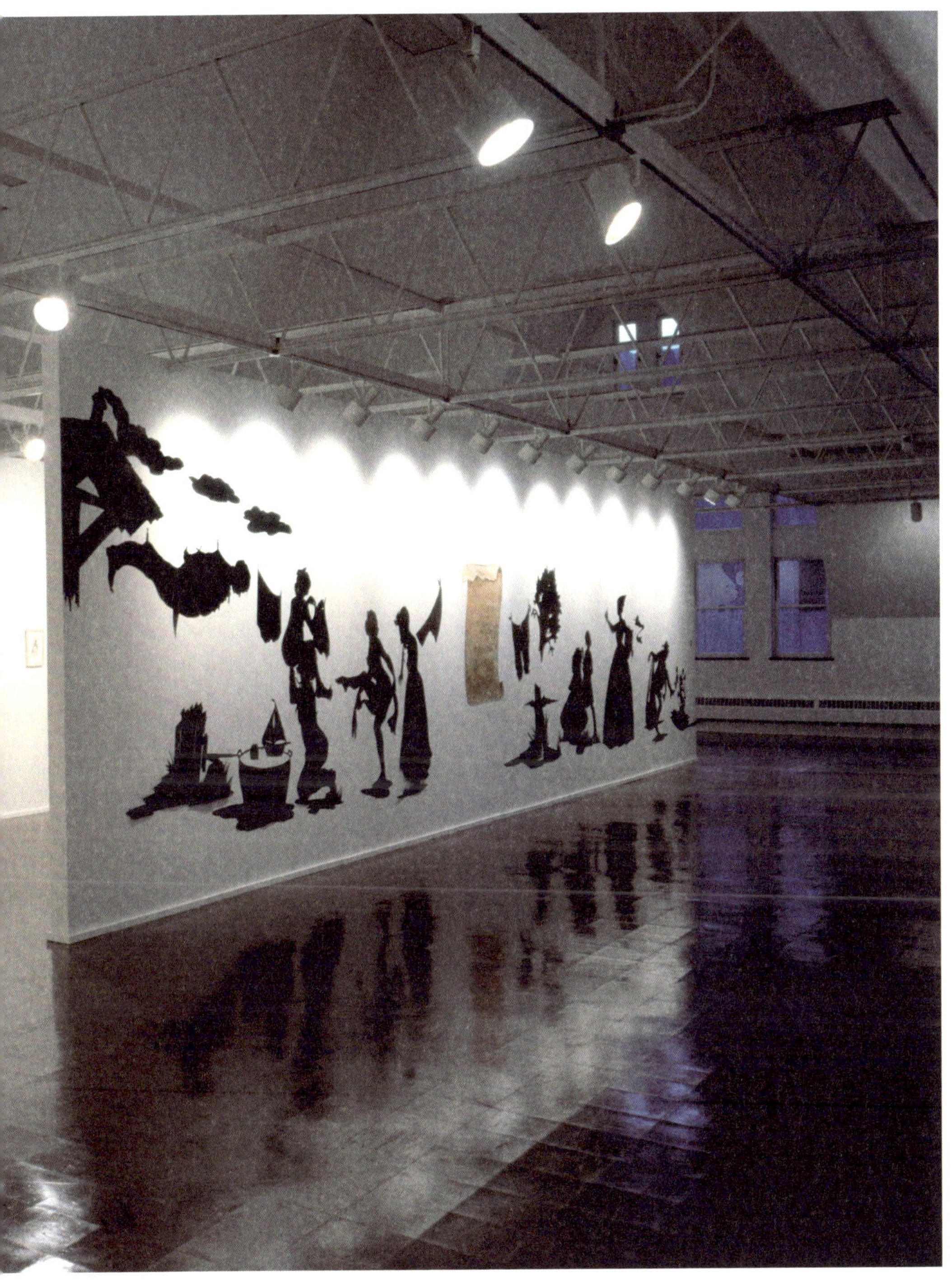

adhesive on wall, and watercolor on paper, 156 × 1,800 inches (396.2 × 4,572 cm). Installation view, The Renaissance Society, 1997. Collection of the MCA Chicago. Photos: Tom Van Eynde

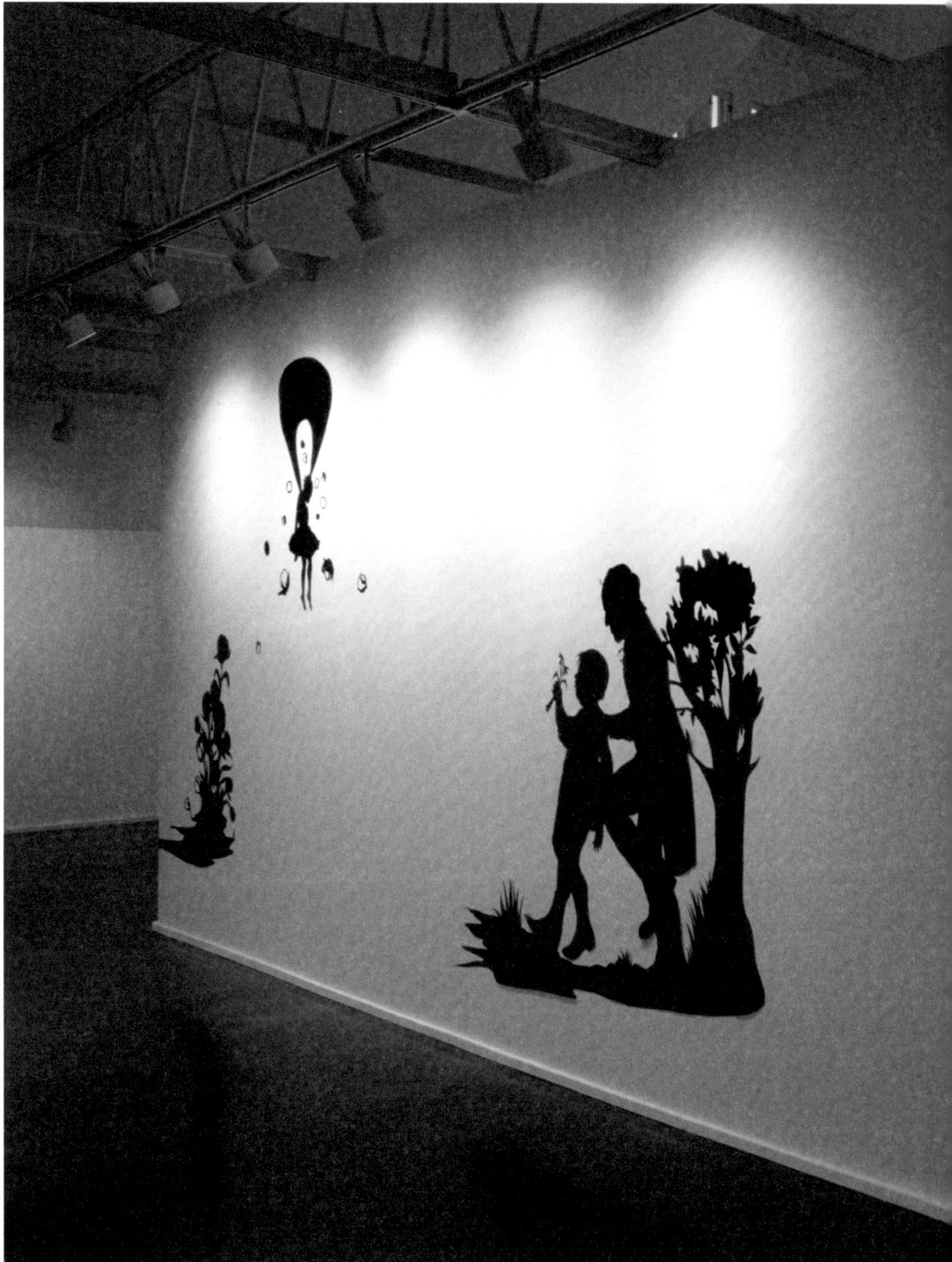

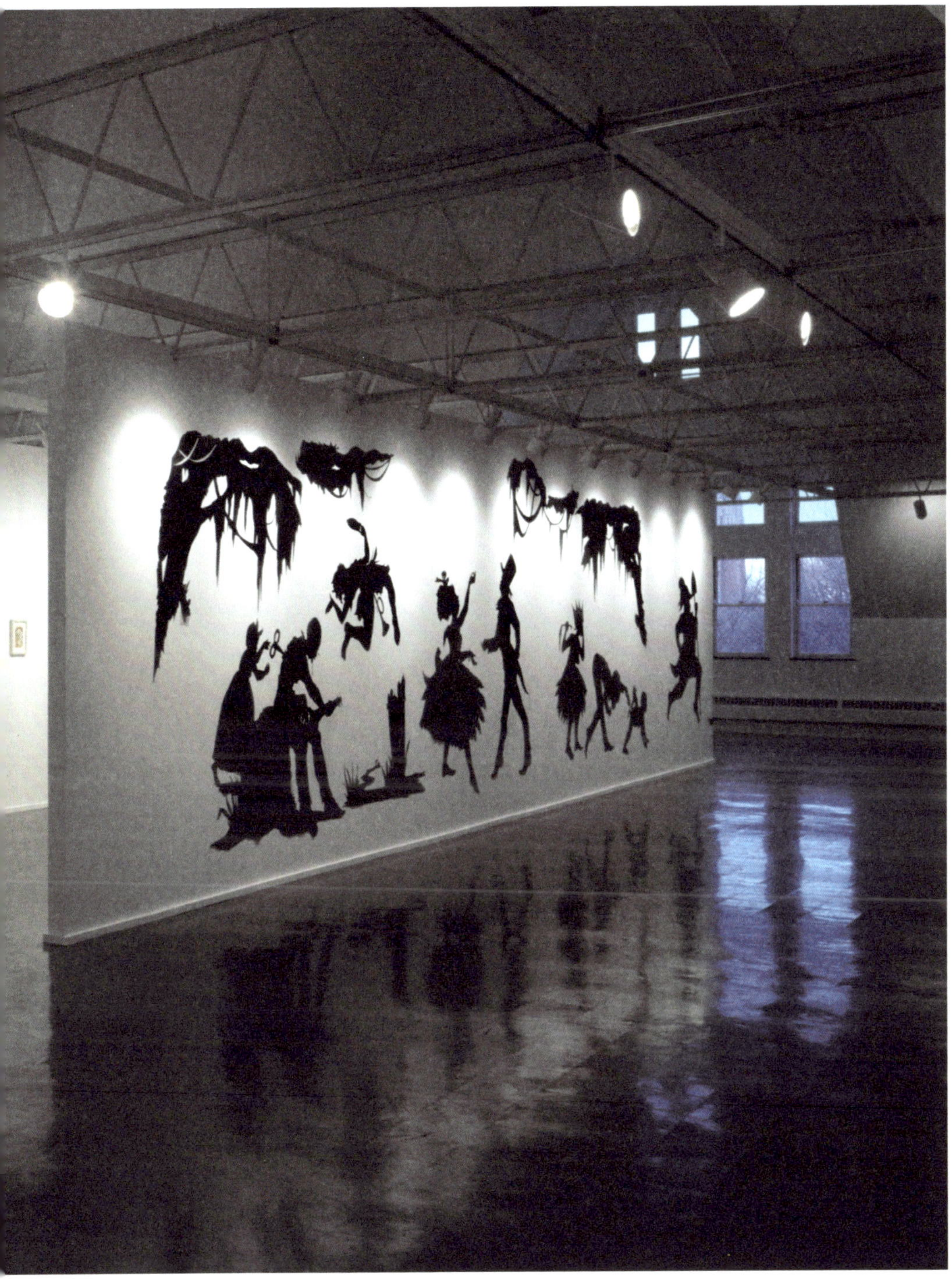

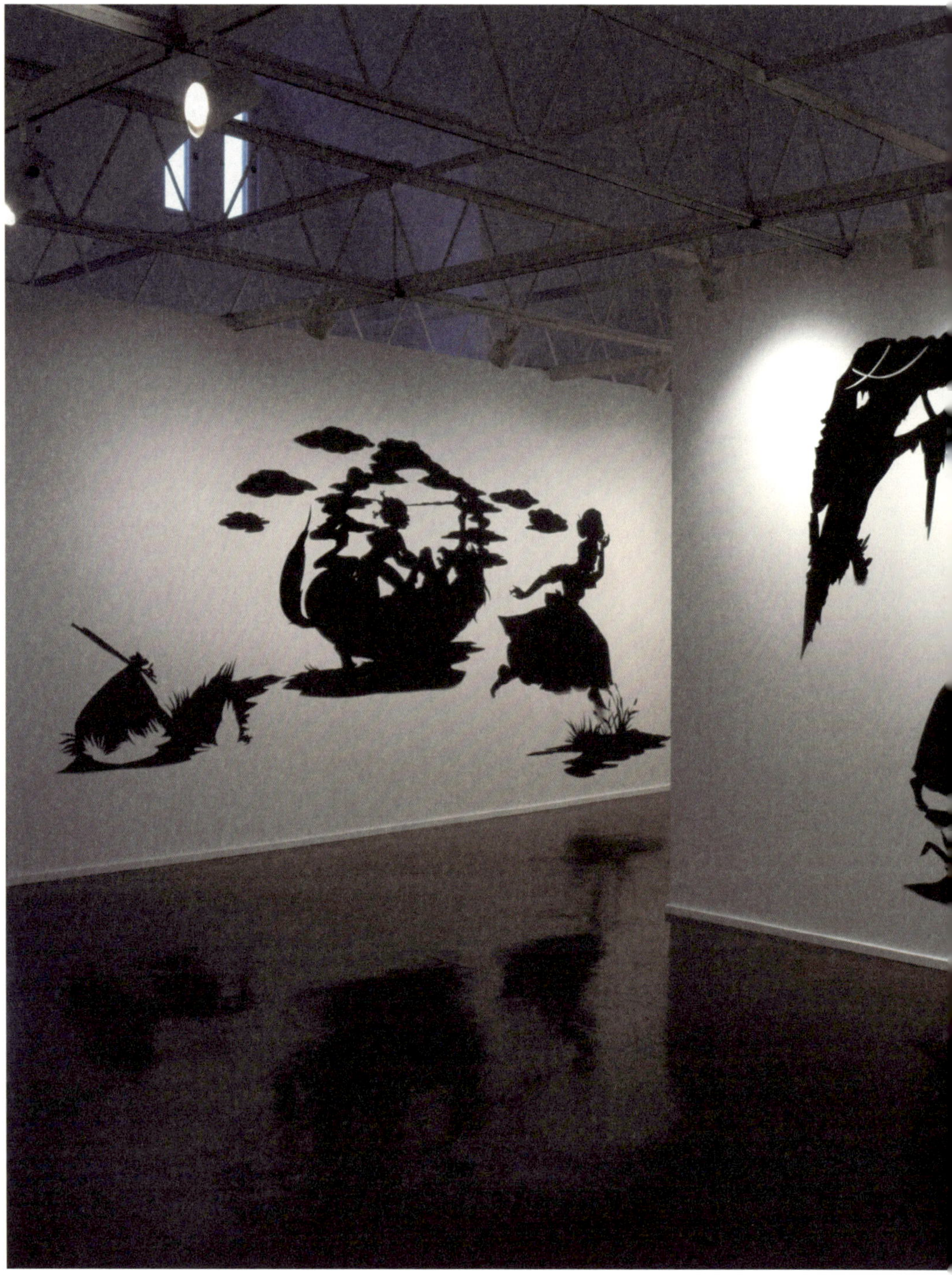

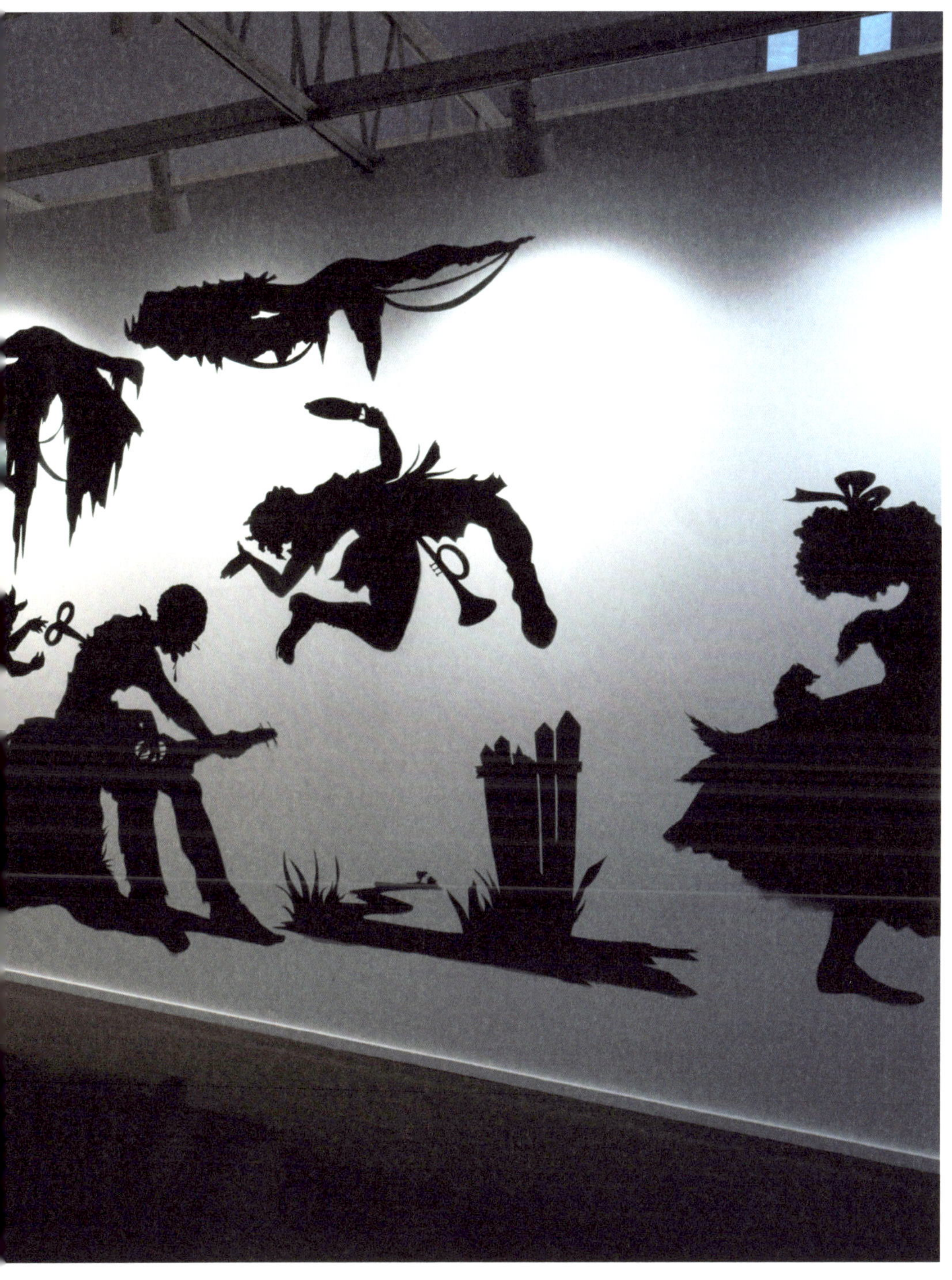

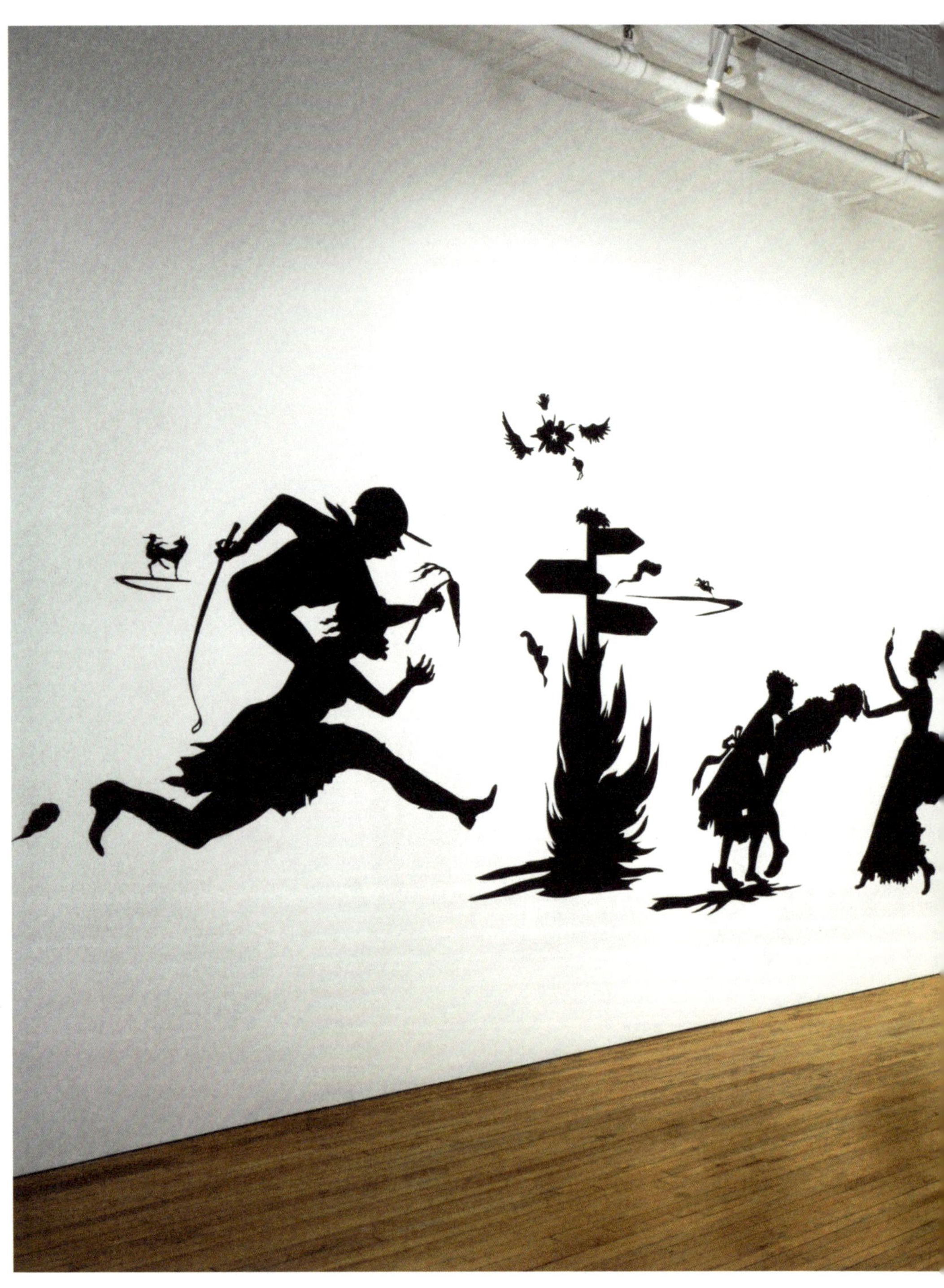

Kara Walker, *Camptown Ladies* (detail), 1998, cut paper and adhesive on wall, 97½ × 666 inches (247.7 × 1,691.6 cm). The Rubell Family Collection

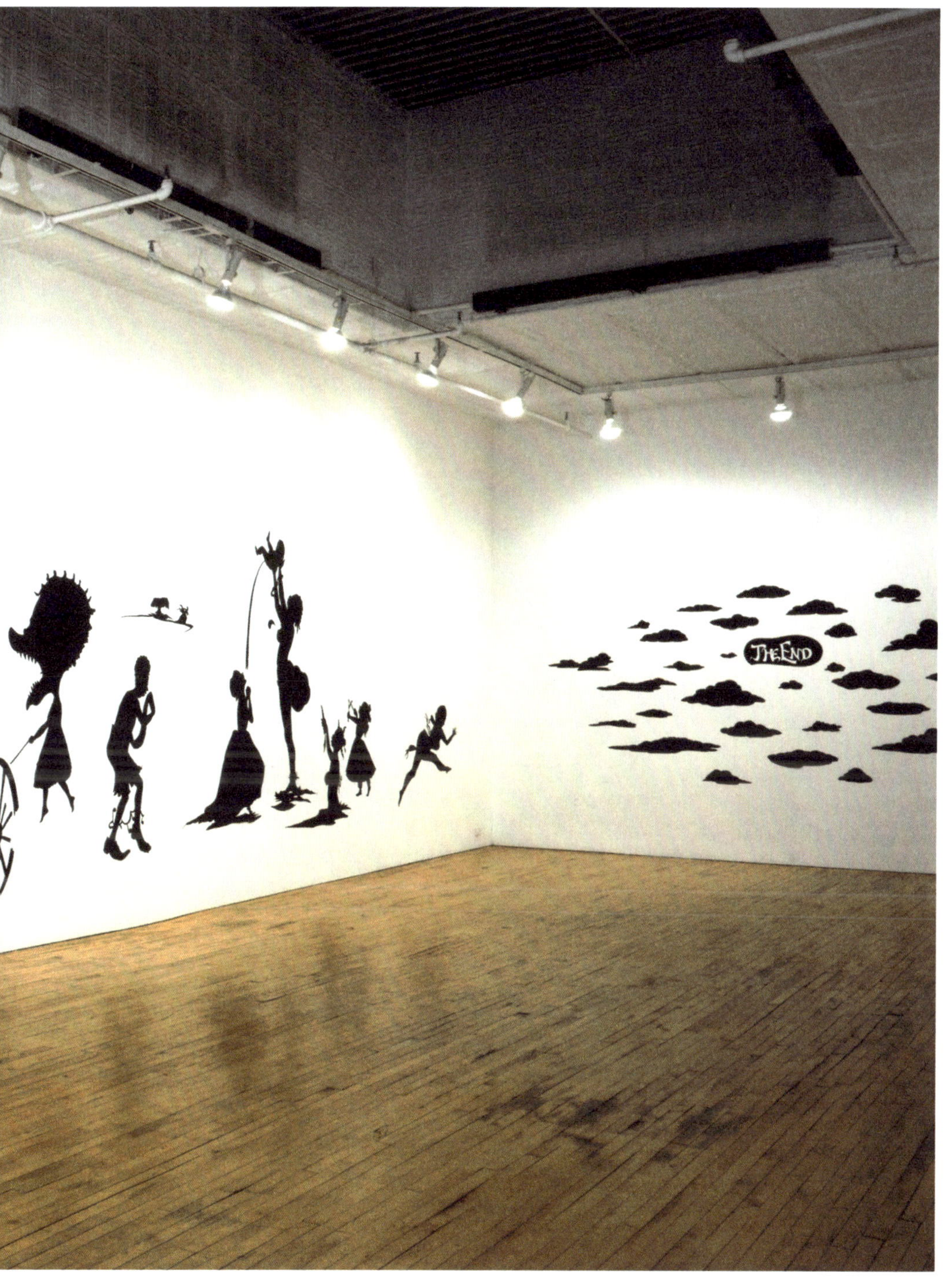
THE END

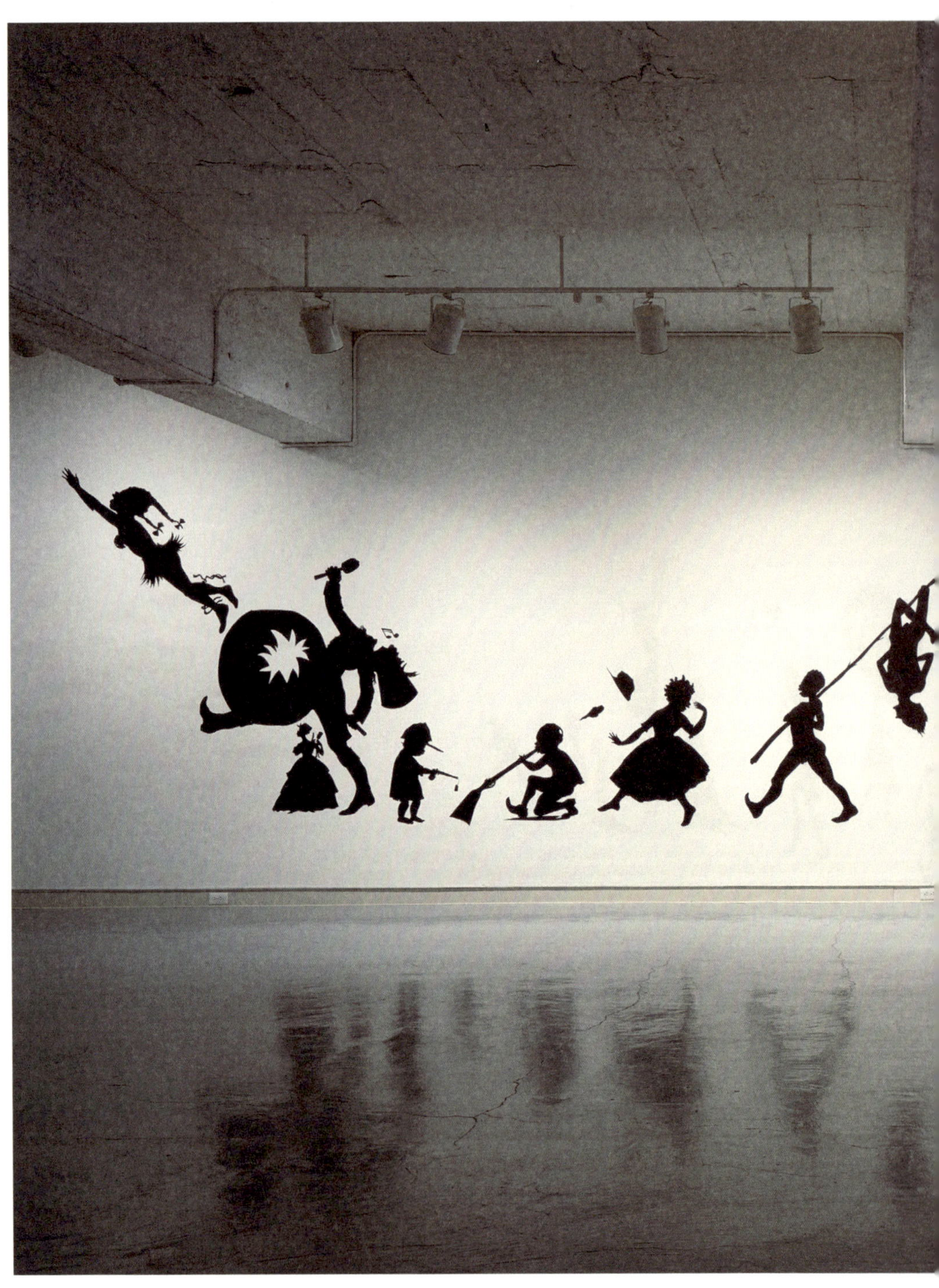

Kara Walker, *Virginia's Lynch Mob*, 1998, cut paper and adhesive on wall, dimensions variable. Collection of the Montclair Art Museum

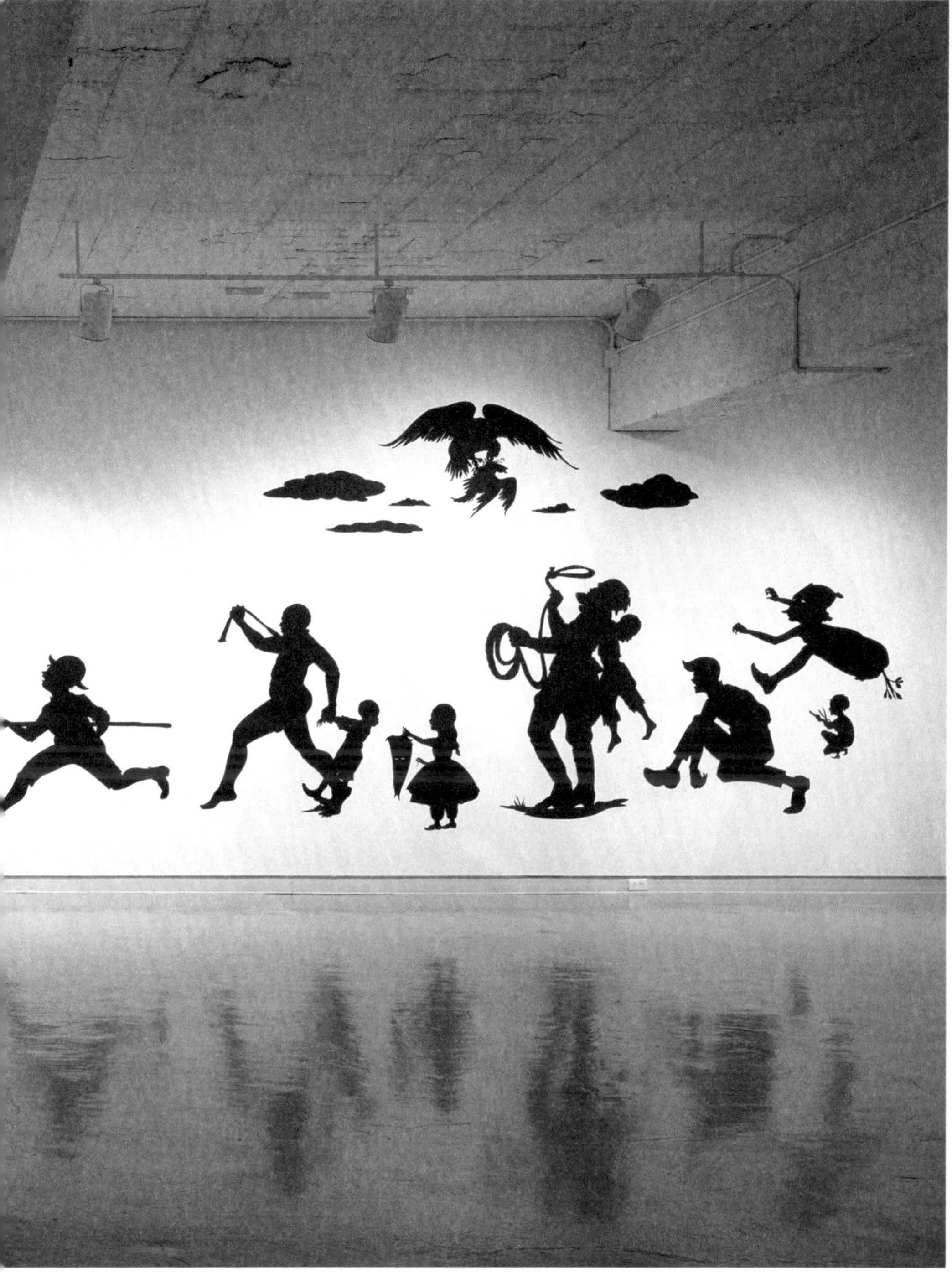

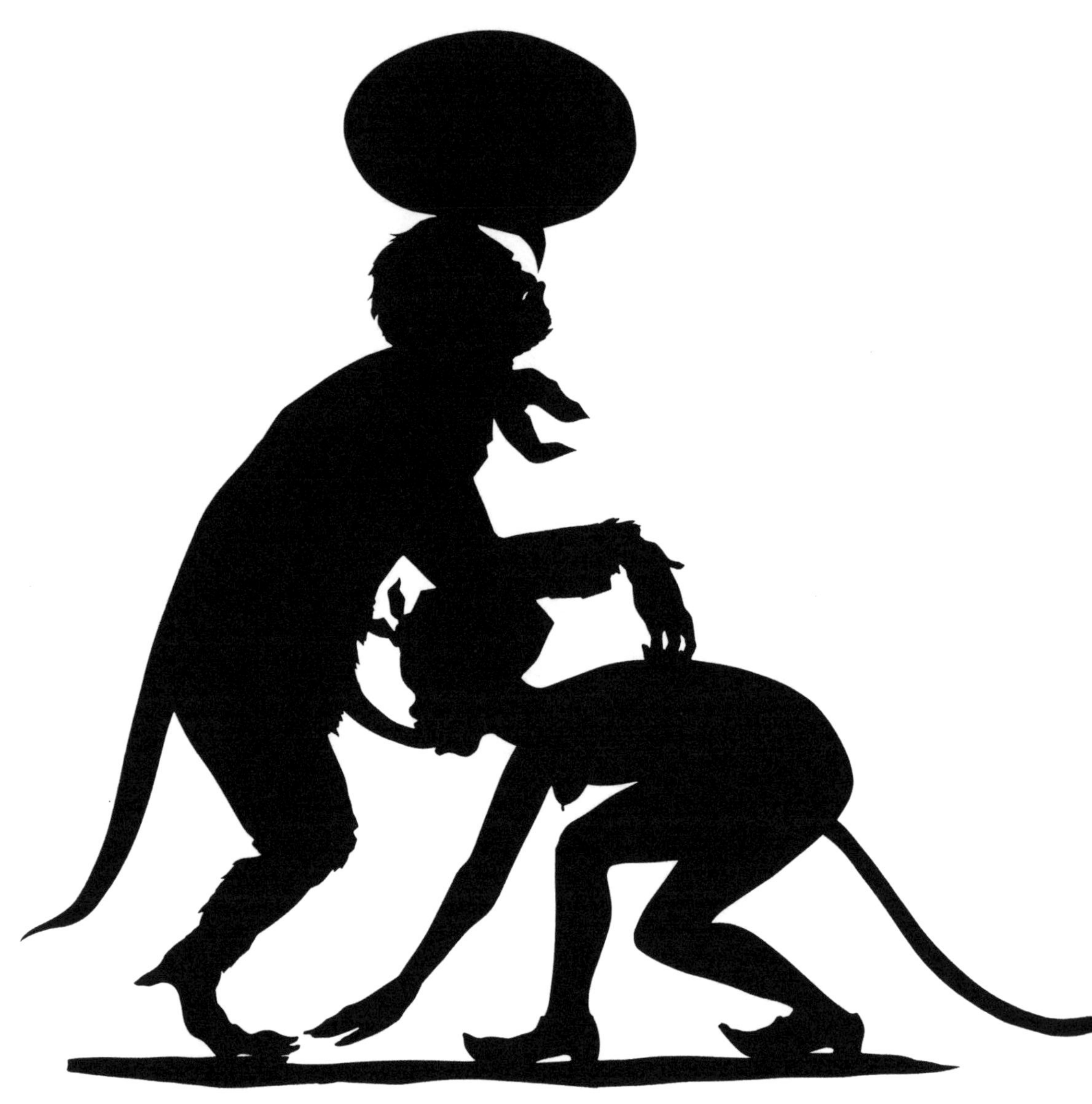

Kara Walker, *Successes*, 1998, cut paper and adhesive on wall, 61 × 65 inches (154.9 × 165.1 cm)

Notes

1 Langston Hughes, "White Shadows in a Black Land," *Crisis* 41 (May 1932): 57, repr. in Edward J. Mullen, *Langston Hughes in the Hispanic World and Haiti* (Hamden, CT: Archon Books, 1977), 90–92.

2 Jerry Saltz, "Kara Walker: Ill-Will and Desire," *Flash Art* 29, no. 191 (November/December 1996): 84.

3 Janice A. Radway, *Reading the Romance: Women, Patriarchy, and Popular Literature*, rev. ed. (1984; repr., Chapel Hill: University of North Carolina Press, 1991), 39.

4 Ibid., 43.

5 Ibid., 88.

6 Alexi Worth, "Black and White and Kara Walker," *Art New England* 17, no. 1 (December 1995–January 1996): 27.

7 Kyle Onstott, *Mandingo* (Richmond: Denlinger, 1957), back cover.

8 Henry Louis Gates Jr., "The Blackness of Blackness: A Critique of the Sign and the Signifying Monkey," in Henry Louis Gates Jr. ed., *Black Literature and Literary Theory*, rev. ed. (1984; repr., London: Routledge, 1990), 285–321.

9 Ibid., 11–12.

10 See Homi K. Bhabha, *The Location of Culture* (London: Routledge, 1994).

11 Saltz, "Kara Walker," 84.

12 "Extreme Times Call for Extreme Heroes," *International Review of African American Art* 14, no. 3 (1997): 8.

13 Hunter Drohojowska-Philp, "Reframing a Black Experience," *Los Angeles Times*, October 31, 1999, 59.

14 Gilles Deleuze and Félix Guattari, "Introduction: Rhizome," in *A Thousand Plateaus: Capitalism and Schizophrenia*, trans. Brian Massumi (Minneapolis: University of Minnesota Press, 1987), 3–25.

15 This discussion of the creation of the Confederate Memorial comes from Gerald W. Johnson, *The Undefeated* (New York: Minton, Balch, 1927).

16 Saltz, "Kara Walker," 84.

17 Ibid., 82–83.

18 Frantz Fanon, *Black Skin, White Masks*, trans. Charles Lam Markmann (New York: Grove Weidenfeld, 1967), 145.

19 W. E. B. Du Bois, *The Souls of Black Folk: Essays and Sketches*, rev. ed. (1903; repr., New York: Fawcett, 1961), 16–17.

20 Saltz, "Kara Walker," 84.

21 Liz Armstrong, "Kara Walker Interviewed by Liz Armstrong 7/23/96," in Richard Flood, *No Place (Like Home)* (Minneapolis: Walker Art Center, 1997), 104. In this passage, Walker refers to her reading of Ann Petry's *The Narrows* and its theory that the racist mind can be understood in terms of one's refusal to participate in stereotypical forms of behavior.

22 Lynn Gumpert, "Kara Walker: Anything but Black and White," *Art News* 96, no. 1 (January 1997): 136.

23 Umberto Eco, *Travels in Hyperreality: Essays*, trans. William Weaver (New York: Harcourt Brace, 1986).

24 Jean Baudrillard, *For a Critique of the Political Economy of the Sign* (St. Louis: Telos Press, 1981).

25 Joel Williamson, *New People: Miscegenation and Mulattoes in the United States* (New York: Free Press, 1980), 63.

26 Catherine Clinton, *The Plantation Mistress: Woman's World in the Old South (*New York: Pantheon Books, 1982), 199.

27 Gates, "Blackness of Blackness," 315.

28 Armstrong, "Kara Walker Interviewed," 106.

29 Worth, "Black and White," 27.

30 For a thoughtful analysis of the incendiary power of this word, see Randall Kennedy, *Nigger: The Strange Career of a Troublesome Word* (New York: Pantheon Books, 2002).

31 Roland Barthes, "The Death of the Author," in *Image – Music – Text*, trans. Stephen Heath (New York: Hill & Wang, 1977), 142–48.

32 Sander L. Gilman, *Difference and Pathology: Stereotypes of Sexuality, Race, and Madness* (Ithaca, NY: Cornell University Press, 1985).

33 Ibid., 15.

34 Ibid., 23.

35 Ibid., 23.

36 Ibid., 26.

37 Plato, *Cratylus, Parmenides, Greater Hippias, Lesser Hippias*, ed. H. N. Fowler (Cambridge, MA: Harvard University Press, 1926), 165.

38 Jacques Lacan, *The Four Fundamental Concepts of Psycho-Analysis*, trans. Alan Sheridan, ed. Jacques-Alain Miller (New York: W. W. Norton, 1978).

39 Gilman, *Difference and Pathology*, 12.

40 Justus Buchler, *Philosophical Writings of Peirce* (New York: Dover Publications, 1955).

41 Saltz, "Kara Walker," 82.

42 Pliny the Elder, *Natural History*, trans. John Bostock and H. T. Riley (London: Henry G. Bohn, 1855), 151.

43 J. Knowles, ed., *The Life and Writings of Henry Fuseli*, vol. 2 (London: Colburn and Bentley, 1931), 26–27, as cited in Victor I. Stoichita, "Johan Caspar Lavater's Essay on Physiognomy and the Hermeneutics of Shadow," trans. Anne-Marie Glasheen, *Res* 31 (Spring 1997):130.

44 Saltz, "Kara Walker," 82.

45 Ibid., 82.

46 Victor I. Stoichita, "Johan Caspar Lavater's Essay on Physiognomy and the Hermeneutics of Shadow," trans. Anne-Marie Glasheen, *Res* 31 (Spring 1997): 133.

47 Adelbert von Chamisso, *Peter Schlemihl*, trans. Sir John Bowring, rev. ed. (1861; repr., Columbia, South Carolina: Camden House, 1993).

48 Hans Christian Anderson, "The Shadow" (1847) in Italo Calvino, ed., *Fantastic Tales: Visionary and Everyday* (New York: Pantheon Books, 1997), 315–29.

49 Ibid., 317.

50 Ibid., 320.

51 Ibid., 325.

52 Ibid., 326.

53 Ibid., 328.

54 The tragedy of this plight is the subject of Spike Lee's harsh satire *Bamboozled*, which updates this situation in terms of a New Millennium Minstrel Show featuring a number of well-known stereotypes.

55 Susan Grubar, *Racechanges: White Skin, Black Face in American Culture* (New York: Oxford University Press, 1997), 95.

56 See Julia Szabo, "Kara Walker's Shock Art," *New York Times Magazine*, March 23, 1997, 49, in which Walker describes her work as a minstrel show.

57 Ibid.

# Index